Finding Katya

*How I Quit Everything to
Backpack the Former Soviet States*

KATIE R. AUNE

Finding Katya Copyright © 2023 by Katie R. Aune.

ISBN: 979-8-9883659-0-7

All rights reserved. This book or any portion thereof may not be reproduced or used in any manner whatsoever without the express written permission of the author except for the use of brief quotations in a book review.

Disclaimer: This book is a travel memoir. It reflects the author's present recollections of experiences over time. Some names and characteristics have been changed, some events and timelines have been compressed, and some dialogue has been recreated. Descriptions of places are accurate as of the time they were visited. Place names in Ukraine have been updated to reflect the Ukrainian spellings.

Designed by Bruce Tria.
Printed in the United States of America.

*Dedicated to my grandmother,
Violet Laven Dalton*

*You go away for a long time and return a different person—
you never come all the way back.*
—Paul Theroux

Contents

	Introduction	3
	Part One: August-November	5
1	St. Petersburg	7
2	Moscow	27
3	Siberia	41
	Part Two: December-May	59
4	Latvia & Lithuania	61
5	Warsaw	74
6	Belarus	84
7	Ukraine	98
8	The Black Sea and Georgia	117
9	Armenia	131
10	Turkey and Georgia (Again)	145
11	Azerbaijan	163
12	Armenia (Again)	181
	Part Three: June-September	191
13	Tajikistan	193
14	Uzbekistan	208
15	Turkmenistan	220
16	Kazakhstan	235
17	Kyrgyzstan	248
	Epilogue	263
	Acknowledgments	273
	About the Author	277

Finding Katya

Introduction

My maternal grandmother, Violet Laven Dalton, wrote the essay below as a college freshman in 1947:

> I must admit that I am only a make-believe gypsy. My forefathers would be horrified at this description, for they were hard-working, steadfast Swedes. I cannot account for my vagabond characteristics, but I have always had a desire to travel extensively and to do unusual things.
>
> I spent my childhood days in a quiet residential district of a mid-western city. It was a pleasant, happy time, but I cannot recall any exciting adventures. As I became older, books opened a new way of adventure for me. Names and places which had been only hazy figures in my mind now became real and definite. Books of faraway places were my favorites. New York, Washington, California, Paris, Singapore, Moscow—all of these were places of glamour. I was interested in biographies of famous people who had accomplished much. Time which should have been used in study or other pursuits was spent in reading and daydreaming.

> *Books satisfied me to a certain extent, but they also gave me a deeper desire to see the world.*
>
> *There is much to anticipate, for I believe that there is a future for the individual with vagabond tendencies. Vast strides have been made in transportation facilities. With aeroplane travel, Europe can be seen on a two weeks' vacation. Bermuda, South America and India will be remote places no longer but the destinations of the ordinary traveler. Surely a make-believe gypsy can ask nothing more.*

Sixty-four years later, in August 2011, I boarded an "aeroplane" not for a two-week vacation, but to start a 13-month journey through all 15 states of the former Soviet Union. I was almost 35 years old and several years into my second career when I quit my job in Chicago, sold my belongings, and set out on what I hoped would be a life-changing adventure.

Just as my Grandma Dalton longed to travel extensively and do unusual things, I pursued an unconventional path to find myself and discover my purpose. What I realized somewhere between Siberia and the 'Stans was that travel can be a lot like life: full of joy and heartbreak, triumph and struggle, happiness and disappointment. Travel may not always live up to your expectations, but that doesn't mean that the journey isn't worthwhile. As I spent more than a year traveling through the former Soviet states, I discovered how much I didn't know—about the places I was visiting and about myself. It wasn't until I started writing this book that I was able to truly appreciate how I evolved throughout my trip. I'd like to think Grandma Dalton would be proud.

PART ONE
August-November

PART 1: AUGUST–NOVEMBER

RUSSIA

Tallinn · Saint Petersburg · Moscow · Kazan · Yekaterinburg · Irkutsk · Ulan-Ude · Vladivostok

ESTONIA

1
St. Petersburg

I bit my lower lip and turned away from the driver.

"*My priyekhali*," he said flatly in Russian. We've arrived.

In front of me was the house I would call home for the next month. I didn't want this stranger to see my lip quivering or the tear forming in the corner of my eye. As I snuck a glance in his direction, he slowly shook his head, and his eyes met mine. In those seconds, I imagined he wanted to say, "I'm sorry I'm leaving you here." I quickly turned to look at the Blackberry in my right hand. An hour and a half had passed since we left St. Petersburg's Baltic Station.

The burly driver, who spoke no English, had been waiting for me when I stepped off the bus from Tallinn, Estonia. The Connecticut-based organization I was volunteering with arranged for him to be there. Relieved at his presence and thrilled to finally be in Russia, I heaved my 60-liter backpack into the trunk of his car and hopped into the passenger seat. I stared back at the station building with "Baltiyskiy Vokzal" spelled out in royal blue Cyrillic letters and smiled. Yes, I was really in Russia.

After slowly navigating the crowded streets of the city

of six million people, we were soon on the outskirts of St. Petersburg. My enthusiasm gradually shifted to nervousness as the buzz of the city faded away. Then, the exhaustion of my seven-hour bus ride started to set in, and I dozed off. When I awoke, we were slowing down to exit the freeway. After turning onto a bumpy, single-lane road, we followed a set of train tracks that disappeared underneath rows of towering pine trees. I didn't see any signs of civilization until we turned left onto a dirt driveway that led to this house.

A woman with a short brown bob who looked about my age walked out to greet me. A yappy black terrier followed close behind.

"*Zdravstvuitye*," she said with a half-smile on her face as she reached out to shake my hand.

"Katya. Welcome. I am Sveta," she greeted me in English before rattling off some Russian to the driver.

He sheepishly nodded to me, returned to the car, and drove off.

Sveta picked up my small backpack and waved at me to follow her. I threw my larger pack over one shoulder as she led me into a house that looked nothing like the pictures I'd received when I was back home in Chicago. Those pictures showed a white stucco home with large bay windows on either side of a small front porch. Those photos featured a modern yet cozy home with glistening wood floors, bright white walls, and a bathroom with a deep jacuzzi tub. But now I was walking toward a shabby wooden house painted red, green, and yellow. Sveta opened the front door—only a screen door, not a true front door—to reveal a foyer filled to the ceiling with cardboard boxes, children's toys, piles of clothing and bedding, small appliances, and even a bicycle. I struggled to maneuver past it all with my pack, not wanting to cause an avalanche by knocking something out of place.

Sveta walked quickly and said little, giving me a tour that was a blur of creaky stairs, broken windows, and an outhouse in the backyard. Our last stop was my room on the ground floor. It was in a section of the house that was separate from the kitchen and the other bedrooms. The room was no more than a three-season porch with a wall of stained-glass windows looking out at the driveway. Another set of windows, half-covered with gauzy white curtains, faced the stairs that separated the two parts of the home. I later noticed that one of the windows had a large hole in the lower corner, allowing flies to come and go. It was only then that Sveta acknowledged the obvious: the house was under renovation.

My head was spinning with confusion. I had signed up months earlier to volunteer in Russia as an English tutor. My contact in Connecticut worked with a St. Petersburg-based language school to arrange this homestay. In exchange for room and board, I would spend 15 hours a week tutoring Sveta's family in English. Shortly before I left Chicago in August, I received the photos of their home, together with family pictures and a welcome letter from Sveta. Her letter mentioned three children, two dogs, and a cat. She boasted of their home's proximity to St. Petersburg and unlimited internet. My journey from the bus station to this ramshackle house made it clear that the city was not a

"20-minute marshrutka ride away," as her letter stated. What happened? And where was I?

There was no time to dwell on those questions as Sveta beckoned me to follow her. After a series of turns and a climb up a steep, rickety staircase, we arrived in a makeshift kitchen on the second floor. Sveta pulled out a chair for me at a plastic folding table in the middle of the room and poured me a cup of tea.

Now, I would meet the rest of the family. I tried to smile as she introduced me to 16-year-old Vanya, 15-year-old Dasha, 14-year-old Sasha, 11-year-old Phillip, nine-year-old Misha, and baby Paulina. It was hard to hide my bewilderment as Sveta's letter had only mentioned three children. Where did Vanya, Sasha, and Paulina come from? I thought it would be rude to ask, so I just nodded and sipped my tea.

Sveta and I made small talk, mostly in English, as Dasha proudly presented me with my dinner: tomato and cucumber salad, lukewarm chicken soup, and boiled potatoes. I hadn't noticed my stomach rumbling, but as I poked at a cucumber on my plate, I realized I'd eaten nothing in nearly 12 hours.

Finally, it was time to return to my room. Sveta brought me sheets and blankets for the bed, which was an L-shaped pull-out couch. As she said good night, she told me she would drive me into the city the next morning to visit the language school. I needed to register for my Russian class. I also needed to get cash and buy a SIM card for my unlocked Blackberry, two things I realized I should have done before I left the bus station.

As I turned on my laptop, I discovered there was not,

in fact, unlimited internet. There was no internet at all. I thought I was an experienced traveler, but I'd never felt so lost and unprepared. Overcome with angst, I crawled under a thick, yet damp, blanket on the pull-out couch and let tears cascade down my cheeks. I had looked forward to visiting Russia for as long as I could remember. Now that I was finally there, all the excitement had drained from my body. Was my dream turning into a nightmare? What had I gotten myself into?

* * *

A week later, I awoke to the feeling of soft black fur rubbing my neck. Tiny claws grabbed at my hair. I snuggled under two layers of thick blankets on a twin-size bed in a new room that I now shared with a small kitten named Chyornish. The large room with walls of windows covered by thick, floral curtains offered privacy but little warmth. I sat up slowly and reached to flip on the white plastic space heater near the foot of the bed, staying under the covers until it glowed bright orange. The heater was a godsend as I tried to study Russian or read my Kindle in the evenings, but it looked like it might spontaneously combust if I left it on overnight.

As Chyornish ran away to find his breakfast, I stuffed soap and shampoo, a towel, and a change of clothes into a plastic shopping bag. With my headlamp around my neck, I tiptoed softly through the hall and into the foyer. The door stood wide open, and the breeze from the nearby Gulf of Finland chilled me to the bone. Light from the full moon peaked through as I tried to navigate the uneven wood floor, using my headlamp to guide me. I slowly walked down three steps past the sleeping black terrier named Maverick and through the carport until I reached the other side of the house. There, a temporary sink stood next to a washing machine. The sink in the kitchen did not work, so this was the place to wash dishes, wash my face, and brush my teeth.

From there, I trudged outside into the muddy backyard. After using the outhouse, I reluctantly knocked on the door of the small wooden building a few feet away. Inside was a traditional Russian sauna known as a *banya*, as well as the family's only shower. A disheveled man who I only knew to be a family friend came to the door. He glared at me and grunted as he let me in. As usual, I'd awoken him. I tried to ignore his obvious annoyance and slipped into the shower room as quickly as possible. It brought back memories of my teenage years, trying to get in and out of our only bathroom before my stepfather could scold me for taking too long.

After showering, I went upstairs to the kitchen to make myself oatmeal for breakfast. Although the homestay arrangement required that Sveta's family provide me three meals a day (and they were getting paid to do so), I quickly realized I was on my own. I have Celiac disease, an autoimmune disorder that is characterized by an intolerance to gluten, a protein found in wheat, rye, and barley. Only diagnosed a year before arriving in Russia, I was still adjusting to a diet without bread, pasta, cake, or cookies. Living in a country where no one knew what Celiac or gluten were posed a challenge. Oatmeal became my go-to breakfast, and

I just hoped every morning that there would be enough milk and sugar left in the kitchen to flavor it.

"How are you, Kate?"

I heard Phillip's voice behind me. He was the only one in the family who called me by my English name. Everyone else called me Katya.

"I'm good. How are you?" I responded as I turned around to see him with a large backpack slung over one shoulder.

"Good," Phillip mumbled as he opened the refrigerator, grabbed a tomato and two cucumbers, and stuffed them into his pack.

I'd gotten used to his presence at breakfast. I usually tried to ask about his school and what he was studying, but I always had to switch to Russian as he struggled to understand my English. For reasons I never understood, Phillip didn't attend the neighborhood school with Dasha and Vanya. Instead, he rode the commuter train and a bus to get to his school each day.

Shortly after 8 a.m., I left for the Lisiy Nos train station, rolling up the cuff on my jeans so they wouldn't get muddied as I walked along the side of the road to the station that shared a name with the St. Petersburg suburb I found myself living in. Twenty minutes later, I reached the platform and handed over three 10-ruble coins at the ticket window in exchange for my ticket to Staraya Derevnya, the second-to-last stop on St. Petersburg's M5 metro line. I carefully placed my small paper ticket in my back pocket. I knew the conductor would ask to see it, and I needed it to exit the station on the other end. I learned that the hard way on my first commute into the city. The train was an old *"electrichiski"*-type train, with wooden benches and no lights or heat. Cigarette smoke lingered in the air from the men who gathered at either end of each car to smoke throughout the 30-minute journey, despite the signs warning that smoking was *"verboten."*

At Staraya Derevnya, I left the train station and walked past bread vendors and flower kiosks toward the metro station to continue my journey. Walking with the confidence of having made the trip a few times, I felt like any other commuter. I was just missing headphones and a local newspaper in my hand. After another 30 minutes on the metro, I got off at Sadovaya to switch lines for the last leg of my trip—just one more stop to Nevsky Prospekt in the center of St. Petersburg. Ninety minutes after leaving the house in suburban Lisiy Nos, I arrived at the language school on Inzhenernaya ulitsa for my daily Russian class.

Foreign languages have fascinated me since I was young. I borrowed Spanish, French, and German language books from my elementary school library, anxious to teach myself long before I started Spanish class in junior high. As a fourth grader, I signed up for a pen pal program and exchanged letters with Claudia in Spain and Ana in Mexico. I spent hours with an English-Spanish dictionary trying to compose my notes to them, not yet understanding basic Spanish grammar or the concept of verb conjugation. It wasn't until years later that I realized my words likely read like gibberish. No wonder I only received a handful of letters in return before the mailbox sat empty.

When I got to college, I continued my Spanish

language study while adding Russian to my repertoire. As a Russian and East European Studies major at the University of Iowa, three years of Russian language study was required. Every semester, though, the class was scheduled daily at 8 a.m., a painful hour for a college student who regularly found herself in the library past midnight. The professor was a sharp-tongued Russian woman with a dark red bob named Irina. She was terrifying. Quick to criticize wrong answers, she never provided corrections. She just scolded and moved on. I may have had three years of Russian under my belt when I left Iowa, but I could barely introduce myself, much less carry on a conversation.

My class in St. Petersburg was a welcome contrast. Class ran for four hours each weekday, starting at the very reasonable hour of 10 a.m. Our instructor Maria was kind and encouraging, gently correcting my pronunciation or poor verb choice. My upper beginner level class consisted of me, Tamara from the Czech Republic, Fabian and Ulrike from Germany, and Julia from Austria. Everyone in the group knew basic grammar and vocabulary, but I felt like I was starting from scratch. Russian was a challenging language. Not only did it use the Cyrillic alphabet, with letters that looked a little Greek and that made *shhhh* and *chhhh* and *zhhhh* sounds, but the grammar structure bore little resemblance to English.

The Russian language was also more nuanced. Russian verbs generally came in pairs, with a perfective and an imperfective aspect—a concept I didn't recall learning in English. Adding to the confusion were multiple prefixes that could change a word's meaning ever so slightly. I was surprised and dismayed to learn there were more than a dozen different ways to convey the idea of going somewhere in Russian. To go somewhere on foot was different than to go by vehicle and going away from some place was different than going to some place.

I had a lot to learn in just a couple weeks.

* * *

"*Vy gotovy?*"

I heard Dasha's voice through my bedroom door, asking if I was ready. The 15-year-old and I had started off on a good note, with her asking to sit down so we could read *Twilight* together the night after I arrived. But when I pressed her with questions about what she was reading, she shook her head in silence. When I suggested we meet again the following night, she demurred. And when I spoke to her in English, she only responded in Russian. Thus, I was pleasantly surprised a few days later when she asked me to visit her English class.

Dasha's school was just a five-minute walk from the house in Lisiy Nos. From the outside, it didn't look that different from my elementary school in Minnesota in the late 1980s. Dasha introduced me to her English teacher, Olga, before running off to her first class. Olga's classroom on the top floor of the gray stone building was spacious, with a large white board at the front and desks scattered throughout the room. Posters and maps of English-speaking countries covered the pale-yellow walls. Each desk sat two students, but, as I would soon see, they were rarely all full. Classes throughout the day ranged from eight to 16 students—far smaller than the thirty students in my fifth-grade class.

As I waited for Olga's first class to begin, I thought back to my own school days. I already wore glasses when I started kindergarten in White Bear Lake, a suburb of St. Paul, Minnesota. My thick spectacles combined with a natural bookishness and lopsided blonde pigtails made me an easy target for teasing. Despite that, I was boy crazy by the time I was in third grade, developing crushes on Dave, then Mark, and then Devin, who broke my heart by moving away. I spent recess playing tetherball and doing whatever else I could to fit in with the so-called popular girls, even if it meant shunning the few girls who called themselves my friends. The cool girls—as I saw them—all took dance classes, so I begged my mom to sign me up as well. Unable to afford the fancy dance school those girls attended, I ended up at a subpar, one-room studio that only reinforced my status as an outsider. And while I was a natural athlete, I was not a natural dancer, and the fit of my pale pink leotard made it clear that I also did not have a dancer's body.

I desperately tried to follow the fashion trends of the late 80s, rolling up the bottoms of my jeans and layering a sweater vest over my T-shirt like I saw in the magazines. Tired of my pigtails, I even chopped my hair to a popular yet unflattering, short, layered style that made me look like a boy. It was all for naught when the most popular girl in fourth grade invited every girl in our class to her birthday sleepover, except for me.

In fifth grade, I got a chance at a fresh start when a new elementary school opened across town—in a building like Dasha's school in Lisiy Nos. By the time I arrived in the fall, my hair was growing out awkwardly, and I had braces to add to my thick glasses. I'd developed my own quirky sense of style, getting my ears pierced a second time and donning huge, dangling earrings. I managed to get my first pair of zippered ankle Guess jeans and an Esprit sweatshirt, but new clothes weren't enough for the popular clique to embrace me. That feeling of not belonging would stay with me for years, even decades. I couldn't help but wonder if any students in Olga's classes struggled to fit in as I did.

A loud bell jolted me back to the present. Olga's first class started to file in: about a dozen teenagers dressed in a uniform of dark pants or skirts and white button-down shirts, much nicer than you would find in most American public schools. They didn't have to worry about wearing the right jeans or the popular brand of sweatshirt. At the same time, they seemed to express their personal style through accessories, from neckties to hair bows. It didn't take long for me to see a divide among the students: a large group gathered around one desk, sharing headphones from their MP3 players, telling jokes and laughing loudly. A handful of others quickly took their seats while avoiding all eye contact. I immediately saw myself in the loners and realized the uncomfortable dynamics of adolescence could be the same everywhere, from Minnesota to Russia.

The students stood as Olga called the room to order, repeating after her:

"Hello."

"Good morning."

"How are you?"

"Fine, thank you."

Each class proceeded in a similar fashion. The lessons were hodgepodge and Olga recycled the same material for multiple classes that should've been at different levels. She read sentences aloud, urging students to repeat after her, but most didn't. She gave students words to define and repeat or sentences to translate. Few succeeded. Toward the end of each class, she would bring me up to the front of the room. Then, she would hang up a map of the United States and ask me to talk about the major cities, the weather, the oceans, and the flag. I tried to speak slowly and deliberately, but no matter what level the class was, my words were met with blank stares. Olga usually ended up translating into Russian.

After a morning of classes with pre-teens and teenagers, a small group of six and seven-year-olds came in like a breath of fresh air. They eagerly repeated after Olga and even asked me questions:

"What is your name?"

"What do you eat?"

"Do you like McDonald's?"

"How old is President Obama?"

The penultimate class of the day was a small group of 13-and-14-year-olds. Shortly after Olga brought the class to order, a blond boy sitting near me suddenly flew across the room and tackled another boy to the ground. Olga quickly marched both boys to the principal's office on the ground floor, confidently leaving me in charge of the class.

The students were reading a story about London, so I tried to quiz them about the plot. As most of the room stared at me in silence, one student took pity on me and tried to answer my questions. Whispers and giggles soon echoed around me as I stood helpless in front of the room. I felt the blood rush to my face as I shifted my weight from foot to foot. My mind went blank as I flipped the pages of their English textbook back and forth, trying to stall until Olga reappeared. I may have been 35, but inside I felt like I was 14 years old again.

* * *

Fourteen can be an awkward age, but I felt like I struggled more than most. With glasses, braces and persistent acne, I was the stereotypical dork from every '80s teen comedy. My discomfort at school was bad enough; add in the unannounced and unwanted presence of a dreadful stepfather and I didn't even feel welcome in my own home.

Reading and writing became both my refuge and my window to a wider world. I wrote in my journal nightly, celebrating with myself when Ross said hi to me in the hallway or I summoned the courage to talk to Jeremy at our lockers. I captured my tears on paper when I was shunned in the cafeteria or bombarded with prank phone calls after school. It was around this time that I discovered the biography of Russia's Catherine the Great, thanks to a book report project for English class.

Catherine was born Sophia, a minor princess in what was then known as Prussia. At only 14, she was married off to her second cousin, Peter, who wasn't much older. He grew into a weak man with a thing for playing with toy soldiers and an obsession with his Prussian homeland, something that put him at odds with his aunt, Empress Elizabeth. As was often the case in the 18th century, the marriage was purely political and designed to solidify the alliance between Russia and Prussia.

Catherine was precocious and ambitious. She threw herself into becoming as Russian as possible and quickly won over the empress and the Russian people. She learned how to read people and manipulate situations to her advantage. Her marriage was an unhappy one, and after her husband ascended to the throne, she overthrew him in a coup, riding triumphantly on horseback into St. Petersburg to claim the Russian crown.

As a teenage girl full of insecurities and doubts, Catherine's story mesmerized me. Sent to a foreign country by her calculating and emotionally detached mother to marry a man she would never love, she nevertheless grew into a strong, intelligent woman—an identity I craved. Although our lives were centuries and worlds apart, I felt she was a kindred spirit. I wanted to read more, and, increasingly, I wanted to see the palace she'd lived in and the jewels she'd worn. As the years wore on, I devoured books about Russian royalty: Peter the Great, Ivan the Terrible, and the last tsar, Nicholas, and the revolution that led to his family's slaughter. Russia became an obsession.

* * *

I walked with purpose along the crowded sidewalk on Nevsky Prospekt in the center of St. Petersburg. With two weeks of language classes behind me and one week left living with Sveta's family, I was determined to see as much of the city as possible. As a 14-year-old dreaming of visiting Russia, it was St. Petersburg I pictured: a maze of canals and bridges, streets lined with pink, yellow and white neoclassical façades, the colorful onion domes of the Church of Our Savior on Spilled Blood and the magnificent Winter Palace, home to the famous Hermitage Museum. While Moscow was Russia's capital, St. Petersburg was its window to the West. St. Petersburg was also where Catherine overthrew her husband to claim the throne of Russia, swearing her oath in the Cathedral of Our Lady of Kazan on Nevsky Prospekt before marching to the Winter Palace in triumph. In the same place where she had married Peter nearly 20 years earlier, she was declared empress.

Those onion-shaped domes came into view as I made my way down Nevsky Prospekt and looked up to my right. The church seemed to be floating at the end of a long canal. Built at the end of the 19th century, it marked the spot where Tsar Alexander II was murdered in 1881. While it vaguely resembled Moscow's famous St. Basil's Cathedral, it stood out among the Baroque and Neoclassical architecture that dominated St. Petersburg. As I grew closer, I realized the onion domes weren't just painted in green, blue, and gold; several were covered with geometric shapes as well. Exterior frescoes gave me a preview of what I would see inside. There, I experienced Russian iconographic art for the first time. Colorful mosaics of saints and biblical scenes covered the domed ceilings and walls of the church—more than 7,000 square meters in total, said to be more than any other building in the world. Everywhere I turned, a saint was staring back at me. Artistically, the mosaics were simpler than the frescoes I'd seen at the Vatican 10 years earlier, but with their gold trim and imposing presence, they felt more impressive.

The next day, I made it to the one place I could not leave St. Petersburg without visiting: the Hermitage. I'd walked past the enormous museum countless times, trying unsuccessfully to squeeze the entire green, white, and gold building into a single photo. Finally inside, I spent the morning mesmerized by the opulence before me. Black marble columns in one room gave way to intricate geometric flooring in the next and fresco-covered ceilings in another. A blood-red hallway displayed portraits of Russian royalty and military heroes. Gilded gold columns lined the grand ballroom while bronze chandeliers dangled from the ceiling. I tried to imagine Catherine walking the same corridors and gliding effortlessly across the parquet dance floor.

After lunch in the comparatively bland museum café, I met a petite, white-haired guide who introduced herself as "Madame" for a tour of the Diamond Room. Madame described everything as "fantastic" or "gorgeous" as she rambled about Catherine's taste in jewelry, the meaning behind the design of Russian Orthodox crosses, and the story behind a series of jewel-encrusted swords belonging to the Romanov family. I peered closely at delicate pieces commissioned by Catherine from foreign artists—tiny boxes with even tinier portraits painted on the lids, many in honor of her son, Paul. Everything I'd read in books years earlier was brought to life in front of me: agate and gold rings belonging to Empress Elizabeth and Catherine and snuff boxes, brooches, and watches given to the Russian tsars as gifts, some with exquisite enamel paintings, others inlaid with gaudy amethysts, garnets, emeralds, and diamonds.

After such a rocky start in St. Petersburg, my dreams were finally becoming a reality. I couldn't stop smiling. No matter how unwelcome I felt in Sveta's home, I felt like the city was embracing me with open arms. I didn't want to leave, although I knew I was only at the start of my journey.

By early October, the leaves were changing colors and floating down from the trees. The reds, oranges, and yellows provided a beautiful contrast with St. Petersburg's pastel façades and bright blue sky. I wandered through cemeteries past the final resting spots of Tchaikovsky and Dostoevsky, blanketed in seasonal orange and gold. I climbed every bell tower of every church and monastery I could, taking in the cornucopia of colors below me. I spent hours walking along the canals and through the parks, leaves crunching under my feet. While I'd traveled solo before, I'd never had so much time to explore a new city. Even in my adopted home of Chicago, I rarely spent time wandering on my own. There was never time. I always had to be somewhere. But in St. Petersburg, my only deadline was the fading daylight. As a result, I probably saw more of St. Petersburg in a month than I saw of Chicago in 10 years. I couldn't wait to do the same in other cities throughout Russia and the former Soviet Union in the months ahead.

* * *

On my second to last day in Lisiy Nos, Phillip invited me to join him for a walk to the beach on the Gulf of Finland, just a few blocks from the house. While I didn't bond at all with the other children, I developed a soft spot for Phillip, who always seemed a bit lonely. He had also started skipping school, seemingly without Sveta's knowledge. I felt I could relate as I had ditched my fair share of school days as well. Sometimes the teasing was just too much and I couldn't bear the thought of facing my tormentors. How many mornings did I hide in my bedroom closet until my mom left for work so she wouldn't realize I "accidentally" missed the school bus?

After traipsing across several hundred meters of the sandy beach, Phillip sat down on a large log and took off the floppy backpack that was too big for him. Reaching into the pack, he handed me three cucumbers and two tomatoes wrapped in foil. Then he pulled out a portable video player and set it on the log next to him. It dawned on me that this had become his daily routine in lieu of sitting in a classroom. I was honored that he chose to include me. Not a fan of either raw tomatoes or cucumbers, I slowly nibbled on a cucumber as we watched a cartoon playing on the video player.

After about 20 minutes, Phillip abruptly packed everything up and said it was time to go. I followed him along a dirt path into the nearby woods and through a field full of tall, pale green grass and dying flowers. We stopped ever so briefly as he picked a handful of small yellow flowers and handed them to me with a smile. Back out on the winding main road, we walked past more than a dozen sprawling mansions surrounded by high brick walls. The sight of such luxury so close to the rundown wooden house I had called home for the past month shocked me. I had seen none of this during my daily walks to and from the train station. I had been so eager to escape from Sveta's home that I'd ignored almost everything around it.

My heart sank a little when Phillip and I finally arrived back home. I wished we had been able to spend many more days like that together. Despite growing up worlds and decades apart, I felt like I could sympathize with Phillip's apparent isolation. I regretted not trying harder to fully understand his situation. I couldn't help but wonder if he was teased or bullied the way I had been at his age. I longed to assure him things would get better. The sight of Phillip standing at the end of the muddy driveway, waving goodbye, and wiping a tear from his cheek would stay fresh in my memory for a long time.

2
Moscow

I lay on the bottom bunk in my Moscow hostel, buried under a scratchy blanket. My head was throbbing. I clutched a damp tissue in my hand, preparing to blow my nose for the umpteenth time. I heard a smattering of Portuguese all around me. The 20-something Brazilians who shared my eight-person dorm room clinked glasses as they downed vodka shots, getting ready for a night of clubbing. It was a Friday night, and a sore throat that started in St. Petersburg had developed into one of the worst colds of my life. All I wanted to do was sleep for hours, if not days. Unfortunately, my dorm mates from Rio had other ideas. My worst hostel fears were coming true.

Before I left home in August, I'd never set foot in a hostel. I pictured hostels as loud, crazy places where drunken 20-somethings pass out or hook up as they traipse through Europe. The idea of sleeping in a room full of strangers, possibly having sex just feet away from me, did not appeal. As an introvert, the thought of being forced into small talk after a long day of sightseeing made me anxious. When I first traveled overseas at age 25, I already thought I was too old for hostels. As a young attorney at a large law firm in Chicago, I stayed in what I considered to be "budget" hotels, spending no more than $100 a night. But $100 a night was not realistic when I was no longer a lawyer making a six-figure salary. Even $50 a night was not feasible as I contemplated months on the road. Hostels seemed to be my only option if I was going to make my money last.

I stayed at my first hostel in Helsinki, which was my initial stop after leaving Chicago. I'd accrued just enough frequent flier miles to book a one-way flight on American Airlines. From there, I would take a ferry across the Baltic Sea to Tallinn, Estonia, and make my way to Russia as part of a months-long journey to backpack through all 15 former Soviet states. Mindful of my new frugal way of traveling, I took an airport bus to the center of Helsinki and followed the directions to the Hostel Stadion, a hostel inside the old Olympic stadium, home to the 1952 Olympics.

Everything about that first hostel stay in Helsinki pleasantly surprised me: my roommates were not crazy partiers, nor were they all younger than me. I was in a spacious all-female dorm with mostly solo travelers who went to bed much earlier than I expected. The lights were usually out before midnight, and the massive hostel enforced quiet hours from 11 p.m. to 7 a.m.

My next hostel, in Tallinn, was quaint and cozy by comparison, with several four-person dorm rooms squeezed into an old house just outside of the Old Town. The owner spent 15 minutes with me upon my arrival, giving me a tour and plenty of tips for exploring the city. I easily hit it off with fellow guests as we hung out in the living room watching one of my favorite sporting events, the US Open tennis tournament.

Hostels in Russia seemed different. They were usually on the third or fourth floor of an old Soviet-era, cinder-block apartment building. Signage was minimal if it existed at all. Because they were converted flats, the hostels were usually comprised of just two or three small dorm rooms with bunk beds and a common area that might double as a kitchen. There were no reception desks, no house rules, and often no staff on the premises. Worst of all, my Moscow hostel seemed to be overrun with the drunken young adults I'd been dreading.

It seemed like I'd barely fallen asleep when I awoke to the vibrations of club music shaking my bunk. The flurry of Portuguese I'd tried to ignore earlier had returned at an even louder volume. A few minutes later, the door to my room swung open, the yellow light from the common area shining directly on my bed. One of my dorm mates stumbled across the room to use the ensuite bathroom. I checked my Blackberry to see it was nearly 3 a.m. As she returned to the party, I got up to close the door behind her. As soon as I was back under the covers, though, someone new stumbled through the room and, again, left the door wide open. Again, I softly pushed the door closed. By the third disturbance, I was desperate for some sleep but also wanted to avoid a confrontation. I did the only thing I could think of: I got up and slammed the door shut with every ounce of strength I had and hoped they got the message.

* * *

I was up a few hours later to pack my things and head downstairs to wait for my new hosts to pick me up. Just as in St. Petersburg, I had signed up to volunteer in Moscow, paying minimally for room and board in exchange for spending 15 hours a week tutoring English. Unlike St. Petersburg, though, I would be staying with a young couple in Moscow. The emails we exchanged prior to my arrival were a source of optimism. They seemed enthusiastic about learning English and eager to introduce me to their city.

Tim and Olya pulled up in a forest green monster of a car with replica California plates and a country western-themed interior, complete with faux cowhide seat covers. Tim proudly showed it off, revving the engine and speeding along the Moscow freeways at nearly twice the speed limit. I tried to hide my terror as we weaved from lane to lane, passing car after car. Tim sensed my discomfort and laughed every time he stepped on the gas. With each roar of the engine, I grew less excited about the prospect of spending two weeks with them.

Tim was in his early thirties, just a couple years younger than me, about six feet tall with dark brown hair and black-rimmed glasses. In any other situation, I probably would have found him attractive. Unfortunately, he shared both a name and a personality with the stepfather who'd made my teenage years miserable. My stepfather Tim was not so attractive; he was a skinny, frantic man with a pinched nose and oversized glasses who always reeked of Drakkar cologne. He obsessed over his red sports car just as this Tim was fanatical about his green speedster. And my stepfather spoke to me with the same condescending tone as my new host.

Olya was in her early 20s and stood no more than five feet tall and spoke in a high, squeaky voice. She could have passed for a high school student. They lived together in a two-room flat in a new high-rise building in Mytishchi, a suburb of Moscow. It was small but cozy and warm, quite the contrast from the drafty house in Lisiy Nos. My room for the time I would spend with them was the living room, with a pull-out sofa for my bed. A sliding door with frosted glass offered privacy.

Although I was sick, Tim insisted that we go to the Circle of Light Festival in Red Square that first night. For more than an hour, I stood shivering among thousands marveling at a colorful 3D mapping projection lighting up the famous St. Basil's Cathedral, the state history museum, and the Kremlin walls. Tim was oblivious to my discomfort, and I didn't want to disappoint him by asking to leave early. After the show concluded, he insisted on driving us up to one of the highest points in Moscow. Standing at the viewpoint near Moscow State University, we could see lights flickering across the sprawling metropolis of 11 million people. I momentarily forgot how miserable I felt and reminded myself how lucky I was to be there. Moscow was one of those cities that my Grandma Dalton had imagined visiting and now I was living her dream.

Tim and Olya worked during the day, so we planned to do English lessons in the evenings. Unlike Sveta's family, who knew little English and showed almost no interest in learning, Tim could already converse freely. He was interested in preparing for an eventual road trip across the United States, but he didn't seem too eager to learn what he didn't know. Olya seemed earnest in wanting to improve her language skills, but Tim spent our lessons talking over and criticizing her, often incorrectly. He didn't believe me when I tried to explain to him the English word for something in Russian. Instead, he looked up the word on his iPhone and came up with some excuse for being wrong. Perhaps most disturbing, he frequently made racist comments, particularly about immigrants from Central Asia, calling them "our Mexicans."

Olya sometimes skipped work to join me in sightseeing. After more than a month of traveling solo, it was an unusual—and sometimes awkward—feeling to have a companion. While I yearned to make friends during my travels, Olya and I had little in common and what she wanted to show me in Moscow wasn't necessarily what interested me most. I longed to explore Moscow's history and immerse myself in Russian culture. Olya, on the other hand, set out to show me the most popular monuments to Russia's military prowess. We visited Park Pobedy, which honored the Soviet victory in the Great Patriotic War, better known to Americans as World War II. We stopped at the famous Victory Monument, walked around a triumphal arch reminiscent of the Arc de Triomphe in Paris, and toured an open-air display of tanks, rifles, and other military equipment. I had a hard time hiding my disinterest, but Olya didn't seem to notice.

Another day, we went to the Izmailovo Kremlin and Vernissage Market. Designed to resemble the 17th century tsar's palace, the kremlin was home to several small museums. My eyes lit up as we passed a museum dedicated to the history of vodka, but Olya simply shook her head when I suggested we check it out. The market featured endless rows of stalls that sold every type of Russian souvenir imaginable—carved wooden boxes, painted dishes, handmade tablecloths and aprons, and nesting dolls in all shapes and styles. One vendor even sold a series of NFL team dolls. I could've spent hours at the market, but it didn't hold the same fascination for Olya. I returned without her the following week, braving ice-cold temperatures to haggle for souvenirs and practice my Russian. It seemed worth it when I proudly scored a set of Minnesota Vikings nesting dolls for my younger brother after haggling solely in Russian.

When Olya wasn't available to join me, I spent entire days exploring Moscow on my own. I went back to Red Square to see it in the daylight and spent nearly an hour wandering through the colorful St. Basil's Cathedral. I toured the famous Kremlin, surprised to find more cathedrals and churches to visit than palace rooms or fortress towers. I spent a morning solemnly exploring the peaceful Novodevichy Convent and its adjacent cemetery, which was the final resting place of notable Russians like Anton Chekhov, Nikita Krushchev, and Boris Yeltsin. While I normally don't love art museums, I spent an afternoon at the Tretyakov Gallery learning all about Russian art and the progression of Russian culture. I surprised myself with how much I enjoyed it. Another day, the State History Museum on Red Square led me through centuries of Russian history, supplementing everything I'd read over the years.

Yet another afternoon, I wandered along Old Arbat Street, seemingly the only pedestrian zone in Moscow. Lined with overpriced souvenir shops, it was a nice break from the crowded streets elsewhere in the city. A small parade of Russian folk dancers bounced its way down the street, followed by a group of girls running around giving free hugs. As local teens teased and flirted with each other around the Princess Turandot fountain, I longed to trade places with them. Similar scenes played out in my head from when I was a teen, but I was always watching wistfully on the sideline. I was never part of the group. Surrounded by their shrieks and laughs, my body tensed up as if it was 20 years earlier, and the giggles were directed at me. Suddenly, I felt very conscious of the fact that I was alone.

* * *

When Tim and Olya came home in the evenings, we either worked on English lessons or watched movies on the projection screen they set up in the living room. One night was a Russian comedy about a radio station that reported fake news stories. Another night was a Steven Spielberg flick that I somehow had never seen. They also introduced me to their favorite television show—*Breaking Bad*, the American cult hit dubbed into Russian. But for my first Friday night in Moscow, Tim and Olya wanted to take me clubbing.

I hated clubbing. At least, I hated the kind of clubbing that I was sure clubbing in Moscow would be: a dark, crowded nightclub with tall, leggy blondes in short skirts and high heels surrounded by gorgeous men who would not give me a second glance. I hated the idea that some burly bouncer would judge whether I was worthy of entering based on how pretty or wealthy I appeared. Even if I made it inside, I imagined music pounding so loud I couldn't hear myself think, much less talk to anyone. Judgment would flow freely: girls whispering about my frizzy hair and lack of style as we waited in line for a single bathroom stall. Guys judging just about everything else about me as they decided I wasn't worth their time.

That was my experience clubbing in Chicago, which unfortunately comprised a good part of my social life as a 20-something tax attorney. There was no shortage of parties to attend, often at the trendiest clubs in the city and frequently on my law firm's tab. While my friends thrived in that environment, I was relegated to being the unattractive fat friend, included solely to provide laughs or encouragement to my thinner, prettier, and more outgoing companions. I oscillated between feeling like I stood out like a sore thumb—like when a guy told his friend to stop talking to me because I was ugly—and feeling invisible altogether—like when a guy pushed me aside to talk to my friends instead.

So when Tim and Olya excitedly told me about plans to go to one of Moscow's most popular clubs, I was overcome with anxiety. I had heard about "face control" at Russian clubs and how strict they could be about admitting people based solely on looks. I was sure I would not make the cut. I hadn't exercised in weeks, had been eating far too many Cadbury Fruit & Nut bars, and my clothes were snug in all the wrong places—not that any of the clothes stuffed in my backpack would be considered appropriate nightclub attire anyway. I also desperately needed a haircut—and a hair straightener. I didn't even have a proper purse with me, just a shoulder bag that was far too bulky to carry to a club.

There was no saying no to Tim. I squeezed into the nicest outfit I could muster—black pants and a billowing short-sleeved, light pink top. Black ballet flats were a far cry from four-inch heels but were certainly better than my hiking shoes. We left around 11 p.m. to meet up with Tim's sister and her husband, who knew the owner of the club in a large warehouse on the Moskva River. To get by the so-called face control, we carried small plastic bottles with ribbons tied around them, proving to the bouncers that we belonged. It wasn't too crowded when we arrived, but we still crammed ourselves into a single booth: Tim, Olya, and me on one side, and Tim's sister and her husband on the other. I ordered a vodka and soda, hoping a little alcohol would put me at ease. Russians have a reputation for consuming a lot of vodka, so I was surprised when the others raised their eyebrows at my drink and ordered coffees instead.

Even though Tim's sister and her husband could speak better English than Tim or Olya, they all quickly reverted to Russian, effectively excluding me from the conversation. I fiddled with the straw in my drink and feigned interest in looking around the club as I gave up trying to understand the Russian being spoken around me. It was hard enough to comprehend the language when I was in direct dialogue with someone in a quiet environment. Trying to make sense of anything in a rapid back-and-forth with music thumping in the background wasn't worth the effort.

After an hour, the group decided to abandon the booth and move to the dance floor. Not knowing what else to do, I reluctantly followed them downstairs to a separate room with a high ceiling and flashing lights. An American DJ was spinning tunes by Jay-Z, Dr. Dre, and Drake. Dozens of Russians packed the floor surrounding the elevated DJ booth, hands in the air, bodies grinding, sweat dripping.

"I love this song!" Olya shrieked in my ear as the DJ switched to an unfamiliar beat.

"A Russian artist," she explained as she grabbed my hand and tried to pull me onto the dance floor. Olya's smile turned into a frown as I shook my head and jerked my hand away. As she and the others drifted further into the crowd, I held my bag close to my body and leaned against an empty spot on a nearby wall. I already felt out of place in my dowdy clothes and bag that screamed "tourist." I didn't want to draw any more attention to myself by trying to dance. At the same time, I easily could've been in Chicago. How many nights out back home ended with me slipping off on my own because I felt so out of place? The only difference in Moscow was that I couldn't ditch my friends for the comfort of my bed. I had to wait for Tim and Olya to give me a ride home.

* * *

A week later, I sat in the back of Tim's car, staring at nothing but semi-trucks and Ladas ahead of us on the freeway leading out of Moscow. It was early afternoon and about five hours after I thought we were leaving to visit Suzdal for the day. One of the oldest towns in Russia, Suzdal was a highlight on almost all tours of the "Golden Ring"—a series of cities northeast of Moscow that formed the heart of ancient Russia and was central to the formation of the Russian Orthodox Church. Indeed, in the late 17th and 18th centuries, dozens of churches were built in Suzdal, leading to an astounding ratio of one church for every 10 families. The town still boasted 30 churches and five monasteries and convents, including multiple UNESCO World Heritage Sites.

I'd been looking forward to visiting Suzdal since I decided to go to Russia. I researched how to visit on my own using a combination of bus and train. I even contemplated staying overnight to give myself plenty of time to explore. When Tim and Olya suggested going together, I thought it was a good idea, saving me time and hassle. But after leaving more than an hour later than planned, I wasn't so sure.

We weren't on the road for more than 20 minutes when a police car pulled up behind us, sirens wailing and lights flashing. I thought we were pulled over for speeding. As an officer approached Tim's window, I kept my hand on my passport in my bag. Russian police had a reputation for always wanting to check documents, so I assumed he would demand to see it. Tim remained calm, and within seconds, the officer was smiling and laughing with him. To my surprise, he left without asking to see anyone's documents. Tim bragged that the officer just wanted to take a closer look at the car. An hour after leaving home, we made a short detour to pick up a friend of Tim's. Twenty minutes later, we pulled into a gas station for a bathroom break and then, a few minutes later, stopped at another station to fill up on gas. I was aghast at all the stops; road trips back home would never be so inefficient.

Two hours after leaving the Mytishchi flat, we were still on the outskirts of Moscow. We spent another two hours at a near standstill. After some quiet questioning of Olya, who was now sitting in the backseat next to me, I learned it was a holiday weekend in Russia. Everyone and their babushkas were heading out of town. My impatience was growing, but I tried to calm myself by focusing on the fact that at least I was going to Suzdal at all.

Eventually, the massive traffic jam that Tim estimated to be 100 kilometers long started to clear. At first, our progress was slow. We occasionally drifted onto the shoulder, creating a third lane to try to zoom past large trucks. We passed vendors on the side of the road selling everything from fresh produce to fluorescent stuffed animals to American flags. We also passed cars that seemed to have given up and were trying to turn around and head back to Moscow. Once traffic was moving again at a normal rate, Tim accelerated loudly and sped past car after car to try to make up time. As the engine roared, I wondered if I might die in a fiery car crash before reaching Suzdal.

We finally pulled into town as daylight began to fade. After parking near the town square, we rushed past a series of arts and crafts vendors and scurried along the streets, passing more than a dozen churches and, finally, the 14th century Saviour Monastery of St. Euthymius, one of the most important sites in Suzdal. We were lucky to arrive when the bells of the cathedral bell tower started ringing—not just a quick ding-dong but an ongoing melody that lasted several minutes. We stopped to listen and to watch the bellringer in the tower far up above us. That alone was so moving that it almost made the whole journey worthwhile. But as the bells mesmerized me, Tim paced around impatiently.

As soon as the reverberations of the bells ceased and the sun disappeared beyond the horizon, Tim declared it was time to return to Moscow. I frowned, not even trying to hide my annoyance. Although I yearned to stay longer, there was no arguing with him. Just like my stepfather, this Tim could not admit he was wrong or change his mind. As much as I appreciated staying in a nice flat and having hosts who wanted to show me their city, I was relieved to be moving on the next day.

It was sinking in that this would be a tradeoff as I traveled: I would need to balance my need for independence with my desire to connect with locals and immerse myself in new cultures. Finding the right balance would be key.

3
Siberia

"*Nyet*," I said with a glare as I pushed past a throng of taxi drivers waiting outside the Vladivostok airport.

They were all hoping to get my $50 fare to the city center. Still bleary-eyed from my eight-hour overnight flight from Moscow, I wanted to get my bearings. I had no interest in a pricey taxi; I was looking for the bus. My hostel's email instructions told me to take "any bus" to the center. I made my way across the parking lot in front of the small airport, heading toward a single bus in the distance. Before I could reach it, I heard a rev of the engine, and the bus soon slipped out of view. A few dozen would-be passengers remained where the bus had stood. I soon learned that there was just one bus, it ran only once an hour, and I had just missed it.

The ticket office stood just a few feet away. Inside, there was a single cashier window and a group of people ahead of me, shouting in all directions. With only natural light coming through the open door, I struggled to make out the signs in Cyrillic. I couldn't figure out what was going on, but it didn't appear anyone was selling tickets. Back outside, the next bus had pulled up, and passengers started battling each other for position as they tried to get their luggage into the storage space below the bus. By the time I realized what was happening, it was full.

Not wanting to wait another hour, I begged and pleaded with the driver in my best Russian to let me and my massive backpack climb on board. While my Russian-speaking abilities had been questionable to that point, I somehow got my message across, and he relented. Or he just felt sorry for this American tourist who spoke horrible Russian. Being allowed on the bus, however, did not mean I had a seat. Instead, I was left standing in the aisle with my backpack at my feet and my daypack on one shoulder. At every stop, other passengers had to maneuver past me to get off. Forty-five minutes passed before a seat finally opened for me.

Ninety minutes after leaving the airport, the bus pulled up to Vladivostok's main train station, from which I would depart on the Trans-Siberian Railway a couple nights later. At that moment, though, I thought it was the bus station where I would catch a local bus to my hostel. My directions told me to take bus 81 from the station, but the bus 81 that came by was going in the wrong direction. That bus driver directed me to the opposite side of the street, but after 20 minutes, I hadn't spotted a single bus going the right way. With my stomach rumbling and desperately fighting the need to pee, I spotted two older women and asked them in Russian where the bus stop was. With a look of pity in her eyes, one of the women grabbed me by the elbow and walked me to the right spot about two blocks over, in a location that I'm sure

I never would have found on my own. Just as we arrived, bus 81 pulled up, going in the right direction.

"*Spasibo. Spasibo*," I thanked the women before I turned to board the bus. For the first time since landing in Vladivostok, I exhaled.

* * *

Two days later, I easily caught bus 81 back to the train station. In addition to my usual bags, I carried a clear plastic shopping bag full of provisions for the three-night, two-day journey to Ulan Ude: six apples, four bananas (not recommended; they spoiled fast!), two packages of salami, four bags of trail mix, two bags of some powdered sugar-dusted corn puff things, one bag of bacon-flavored potato chips, one box of orange juice, and one large bottle of water. It wasn't the most nutritious meal plan but being gluten-intolerant in a city with just a couple small grocery stores within easy reach of my hostel, my options were limited.

I am the kind of person who arrives at the airport at least three hours before an international flight and then spends two hours killing time because I got through check-in and security in 15 minutes. When it came time to start my Trans-Siberian journey, it was only natural that I would arrive at the station more than an hour ahead of my 10:30 p.m. departure time. I wanted to be the first one in my four-person *kupe* (second class) compartment on the train, so I could get situated on my own before anyone else joined me. While I had once taken an overnight train between Cairo and Luxor in Egypt, this would be my first experience in a true sleeper car, and I had no idea what to expect.

Boarding began around 9:45 p.m. While my backpack got stuck a few times in the narrow hallway, I easily found my compartment. I had a bottom bunk, which I lifted to shove my large pack into the metal bin underneath. My shoulder bag would stay with me on my bed, and my daypack found a place under the small table between the bunks. A silver thing called a *samovar* provided boiling water at one end of the car, a garbage bin sat at the other, and a schedule of train stops was posted in the middle (all on Moscow time, even though the train would cross eight time zones). Toilets with small metal sinks were located at each end of the hallway. I found a rolled-up mattress, pillow, and thick wool blanket on my bunk when I boarded the train, and the *provodnitsa* distributed sheets and a small towel shortly after we departed.

My first "roommates" were a plump, gold-toothed babushka and her 12-year-old granddaughter. Despite having the top bunks, they quickly commandeered the bottom ones to sit at the small table between the two beds. This, I soon realized, was typical; during waking hours, those of us who chose to book a bottom bunk were expected to share. Once they were settled, the granddaughter pulled out two glass mugs, two metal spoons, and two packages of noodles. She disappeared for a few minutes, returning with mugs full of boiling water. Not wanting to interrupt their ritual, I buried my head in my Kindle. Shortly after midnight, the babushka decided it was time for bed. She and her granddaughter moved to their respective top bunks, and she flipped off the light.

As I lay in my bunk, feeling the *ba-dum, ba-dum,*

ba-dum of the train, I thought of my Grandma Dalton. She was my mom's mother, born in Des Moines, Iowa to Swedish immigrant parents. She died of cancer when I was only six, leaving me with no memories of her. But as an adult, I uncovered journals, diaries and essays that she wrote as a young woman. I read them cover to cover, eager to understand the only grandparent I never knew. She was barely 20 when she took the train by herself from Iowa to Seattle—something unheard of in 1938. Indeed, she wrote of being "rather lonely" as the only young person on the train. I couldn't help but wonder what she would think of her granddaughter embarking on a solo train journey of her own three times as long, across a country half a world away.

I tossed and turned throughout the night, finally rising for good when the sun came up, not knowing at all what time it was. When we arrived in Khabarovsk a few hours later, the babushka and her granddaughter gathered their things and disappeared as quickly as they'd arrived.

Just minutes later, a 40-something teacher named Lena joined me.

"*Davayte uznayem drug druga*," Lena said to me after changing out of her street clothes into tie-dyed blue flowing pants and a matching singlet.

"*Da, no ya plokho govoryu po-russki.*"

If there was any phrase I had mastered in Russian, it was telling people I spoke Russian poorly. I wanted to start with low expectations. Lena was a teacher, though, and had more patience than most. After suggesting we get to know each other, she spent the next couple of hours trying to do just that. If I didn't understand her, she repeated the phrase at a slower pace. If I still didn't get it, she found different words to use. We passed my Russian-English dictionary back and forth as a last resort.

The hours on the train passed quickly with Lena. She helped me read my horoscope in Russian, and I tried to explain to her who was in the small photo album I carried with me. That was one tip I'd been given before embarking on my trip: to carry pictures from back home to share with people I met. Lena was the first person who showed enough interest for me to share. Our conversation was by far the longest and most in-depth that I'd had in Russian since arriving. It was exactly what I'd hoped for when I decided to cross the entire country by train, and it raised my hopes for the rest of my Trans-Siberian journey. I hoped to meet many more Lenas along the way.

* * *

I stared out of a dusty window at endless rows of wooden houses as the train slowed to a crawl. The shack-like structures were loosely connected by wires swaying 20 feet in the air. Their brightly painted shutters offered the only glimpse of life. This was my introduction to the town of Ulan Ude, my first stop along the Trans-Siberian. It was 62 hours from Vladivostok.

Home to about 400,000 people, Ulan Ude was the capital of the Republic of Buryatia, which had been part of Russia since the 1920s. Buryatia was in south-central Siberia, stretching from the eastern shores of Lake Baikal south to Russia's border with Mongolia. Its history could be traced back to the Stone and Bronze Ages, and its indigenous people, the Buryats, were of Mongolian origin—possibly even descended from Genghis Khan. I expected Siberia in November to be dark and dreary, but the days I spent in Ulan Ude were bright and sunny.

My hostel looked out over a large open square surrounding the world's largest Lenin head. Vladimir Lenin, of course, was the leader of the Bolshevik Party that seized power during the Russian Revolution in 1917. A controversial figure, he was known both as a champion of the working class and as a violent oppressor of his political opponents. He also developed a cult of personality within the former Soviet Union after he died in 1924. I didn't realize it at the time, but statues of Lenin would be ubiquitous as I traveled through Russia and the former Soviet states.

Not far from the main square, I found Ulan Ude's version of Moscow's Old Arbat Street, a pedestrian-only zone stretching several blocks. I blended in everywhere else in Russia, but my pale skin and blonde hair stood out among the darker-skinned Buryats. For the first time, I felt some stares. I snapped the obligatory Lenin head photos and grabbed lunch at an Italian restaurant before hopping into a marshrutka (a shared taxi that runs on a fixed route) to take me to the open-air Ethnographic Museum on the outskirts of town.

Unlike central Ulan Ude, the museum grounds were covered with fresh snow. I plodded past a traditional wooden church and a series of homesteads belonging to Eastern Orthodox Christians known as Old Believers who followed the Russian Church as it was in the early 17th century. After two months in Russia's most famous metropolises, it was refreshing to wander among the pine trees, breathing the cold winter air and getting a look at the life of rural Russians. Then, to my great surprise, I arrived at a small zoo featuring camels, yaks, wolves, and two very sad-looking brown bears in way-too-small cages. What had been a pleasant excursion around the open-air museum suddenly left me with a bad taste in my mouth.

The next day, I hired an English-speaking guide, Olga, to take me to one of the main tourist attractions in Buryatia: the Ivolginsky Datsan. Located about 30 kilometers south of Ulan Ude, the datsan was a Buddhist monastery founded during Stalin's times and, surprisingly, with his permission. It remains the center of Buddhism in Russia today.

Following custom, we walked around the monastery complex in a clockwise direction, passing a series of red and gold prayer wheels and small wooden houses where the monks lived. We stopped in front of a wishing stone where Olga encouraged me to place my hand on the stone and make a wish. Then, I walked to a line on the ground several feet away. I turned and walked back toward the stone with my eyes closed. If I made it in a straight line and touched the stone again, Olga said my wish would come true. Unfortunately, I missed by a few inches.

Our last stop was at the colorful main temple known as Sogchen. I removed my hat before entering and walked clockwise around the interior of the temple. Olga told me that the altar contained the images of a thousand Buddhas. Standing in front of it, facing golden Buddha statues of all sizes, I was reminded of the brilliant iconostasis in the Church of Our Saviour on Spilled Blood and other Russian churches I'd visited. Despite the difference in religious beliefs, the affinity for gold seemed to be constant. I departed the temple by carefully walking backward out the door so as not to turn my back to the gods.

With our tour of the datsan complete, it was time for tea. Olga shared that she was ethnically Buryat while her husband was Russian. They were both Protestant, living in a region where Russian Orthodoxy and Buddhism were the majority. Olga spoke fluent English and loved meeting foreigners, especially Americans.

"I was too excited to sleep last night," Olga confessed as she refilled my teacup. "I couldn't wait to meet you."

She went on to explain that she thought the Russian government openly promoted anti-Americanism by encouraging jealousy and resentment of Americans. I raised an eyebrow, thinking of how excited the other Olga was to meet me in Lisiy Nos. While her students may have been indifferent to my presence, I never sensed any hostility. I also thought of Tim and his obsession with American culture and desire to road trip across the country.

"I was teaching an English class and one of my students said to me, 'I hate Americans,'" Olga told me. "I asked him, 'Have you ever met an American?'"

The answer, of course, was no.

Olga, on the other hand, had met a lot of Americans. She learned English from American missionaries who came to Buryatia when she was a child. She spent days with American tourists who hired her as a guide around Ulan Ude. Olga longed to visit Europe and the United States. She regretted passing up an opportunity to study abroad in college because she met her husband. The logistics, she explained, were challenging. She would have to travel to Moscow, more than 5,000 kilometers away, just to apply for a visa. That would require either an expensive flight or a days-long train trip each way. She had never been further than Novosibirsk, which was half as far. Since her husband didn't share her desire to see the world beyond Russia, making her dream a reality didn't seem possible.

I thought I knew how Olga felt.

Growing up, my dad traveled a lot for his job in "international sales." He flew off to places that I could only dream of: South Africa, Brazil, Singapore, and Germany. He was sometimes gone for a few days, sometimes for a few weeks. His return usually meant waking up to him turning on the hallway light before coming into the room I shared with my brother. He would leave welcome-home gifts on the nightstand in between our beds, trying not to disturb us. One trip brought a My Little Pony doll, another brought a new Barbie. A return from Asia brought a custom stamp set that allegedly spelled my name in Chinese letters. After one of those trips, there was a globe.

I spent hours examining every inch of the colorful sphere, spinning it and poking my finger at random to see what country I would land on. I filled page after page of college-ruled Mead writing tablets with lists of every country I identified, sometimes organized alphabetically, sometimes by continent. I would read them out loud, intrigued by names like Bangladesh, Upper Volta, and Zaire. I compared lists and then started all over again, never satisfied that I hadn't missed a country. A partial set of garage sale encyclopedias allowed me to read about the places I saw on that globe. Hand-me-down textbooks told me stories of the people who lived in those faraway lands. But visiting those places? That never seemed possible.

Despite my dad's globetrotting, our family trips never went further than camping in Wisconsin Dells or visiting my paternal grandparents in Brainerd, Minnesota. After my parents' divorce when I was eight, my mom began taking us skiing in Colorado over school breaks, but I wanted to be in sunny Mexico like my friends. When I got to college, I flipped through shiny brochures about studying abroad in Russia, but I was working 20 hours a week to pay my way through school. The idea of taking a semester or a summer to go overseas seemed impossible.

As much as I thought I knew how Olga felt, I recognized that I had it much easier than she did. I was privileged to carry a U.S. passport, a document that automatically made international travel more accessible for me. Indeed, as soon as I finished law school with a six-figure job lined up, I booked a three-week tour of Europe and never looked back.

We rode back to Ulan Ude in silence. As Olga dropped me off at my hostel, she asked for my email address, insisting we keep in touch. I smiled when I received an email from her a week later: "After I met you, I have understood that traveling, it is something real. Now I am thinking about traveling to Europe."

Meeting Olga showed me one of the best things about travel: the ability to learn from and inspire those you meet along the way. Just as I hoped to meet many more Lenas on my trip, I hoped to encounter many more Olgas as well.

* * *

The sky was still black as I climbed into the large white van that had just pulled up in front of my Irkutsk apartment building. Nearly an hour late, this was the marshrutka that would take me to Lake Baikal for the weekend. The largest freshwater lake in the world by area, Lake Baikal was also the world's deepest lake. It's probably one of the few places in Russia outside of St. Petersburg and Moscow that many people have heard of. If I'd just wanted to see the lake, I could have taken a day trip to the town of Listvyanka on the lakeshore just an hour away. But I really wanted to visit Olkhon Island, the largest island in the lake. To get there would take five or six hours. As a result, the trip was best as a weekend getaway.

Luckily, I had plenty of time. Prior to arriving in Russia, I had signed up to volunteer with a nonprofit organization in Irkutsk that was building a hiking trail around the lake. Because I considered my trip a temporary career break and intended to find a job again when I returned home, it was important to me to have as many potentially resume-building experiences as possible. I committed to volunteer for two weeks and booked my onward train to Krasnoyarsk for two Saturdays after my arrival.

However, when I got to Irkutsk, I learned they didn't need my services after all. After my lackluster experiences volunteering in St. Petersburg and Moscow, I was disappointed to see an opportunity fall through altogether.

I wondered how much more challenging my job search would be if I didn't have any substantive experience to show for my so-called career break. Putting this letdown aside, I resolved to make the most of the extra free time, just as I'd done in St. Petersburg.

The first thing I did was book a weekend tour to Olkhon Island through a local hostel. It included roundtrip transportation and two nights in a homestay on the island. Beyond that, I had no idea what to expect. As I climbed into the hour-late marshrutka, I squeezed into the only open seat and placed my daypack on my lap. A Belgian couple, Maarten and Mariann, sat across from me and quickly introduced themselves. They were nearing the end of a nine-month honeymoon that had taken them on a route somewhat the reverse of what I had planned. Starting in Jordan, they went through Syria, Turkey, Iran, Central Asia, China, and Mongolia before taking the Trans-Mongolian Railway into Siberia and Irkutsk. I peppered them with questions: "What were the 'Stans like?" "Was it hard to get visas?" "How were the border crossings?" They were the first long-term travelers I'd met on my trip, and I couldn't contain my excitement.

Two older women in heavy fur coats and fur hats sat behind Maarten and Mariann. Across from them was a 20-something girl with jet-black hair, tight jeans, and heels that seemed inappropriate for our destination. Three heavyset men around my father's age filled in the remaining seats that weren't piled high with luggage. Before we'd even pulled away from my building, they were passing around a bottle of vodka. Never mind that the sun hadn't come up yet. It was quite the contrast to the club in Moscow when Tim and Olya opted for coffee over alcohol.

Six hours passed quickly. The ride brought a few surprises. I used my first long-drop squat toilet when we stopped at a roadside café for lunch. There's no feeling quite like peeing over an open hole with a frigid Siberian breeze blowing below you. Inside the café, a flat-screen television played a Russian version of the American sitcom *Married with Children*. At first glance, I thought it was the original version dubbed into Russian or with Russian subtitles. When I looked closer, I saw it was a completely re-made version with Russian actors who looked just like Peg, Al, and Kelly Bundy. It was another reminder of how much Russians seemed to love American culture while allegedly hating Americans themselves.

For the last leg of our journey, the marshrutka drove onto a vehicle ferry for a 20-minute ride across Lake Baikal to Olkhon Island. Mid-November in Siberia meant the ferry had to plow through floating ice chunks just to get to the port. As we crossed, I couldn't help but think that if we sank, we would be sinking into water more than 5,000 feet deep. Two hours later, we arrived in Khuzhir, the largest town on the island. Two of the men were falling over drunk by that point, having spent much of the journey chugging beers and swishing vodka. The marshrutka dropped me off in front of a pink wooden house owned by yet another woman named Olga. After inhaling a late lunch of potatoes fried with dill, fish soup, and a cabbage and carrot salad, I bundled up to explore Khuzhir.

The beach-like sandy streets were nearly empty as I

wandered down the main drag. I passed decaying wooden houses, junkyard cars, and a few grazing cows on the side of the road. A pack of dogs soon joined me and wouldn't leave my side as I strolled along, the sand feeling smooth under my feet. After two months of chaotic, concrete jungles, the simplicity of everything in Khuzhir brought me a much-needed feeling of serenity.

The next day, I split the cost of a driver with Maarten and Mariann to explore the island. We drove up the west coast to the northernmost point at Cape Khaboy and then back along the east coast until crossing over and retracing our path back to Khuzhir. While we departed under a clear blue sky with the sun shining, gray clouds soon crept in. After a stop along the beach, where I dipped a couple fingers in the nearly frozen Lake Baikal, clouds quickly turned to flurries. Those flurries turned into a full-blown snowstorm by the time we reached the cape, where the ground was covered by several inches of newly fallen snow.

We sat in the van as we enjoyed a picnic lunch of smoked omul (the local fish), vegetables, and tea with our driver, Vasya. Then, we hopped outside to frolic in the fresh powder. We tentatively followed Vasya out toward the cape to get the best views, slipping and almost wiping out several times along the way. It seemed incredible that by the time we reached our sixth and final stop—a rocky beach on the east side of the island—the snow completely subsided, and the sun started to peek through the clouds again. Our ride back to Khuzhir was a bumpy one as Vasya carefully navigated around deep, frozen tire treads and through forests of skinny pine trees. By the time we reached Khuzhir, the skies were clear blue.

After warming up with some tea at my homestay, I walked out to a small hill on the edge of town to watch the sunset over the harbor. As the sky filled with every shade of yellow and orange, I closed my eyes and smiled. It was the most relaxed I'd felt since arriving in Russia.

* * *

I trudged blurry eyed out of the Belorusskaya train station in central Moscow. The city was covered with a layer of snow and slush that hadn't been there a month earlier. I stepped carefully over ice patches as I walked a few blocks to my new hostel, hoping they would have room for me so early in the morning. I was used to this by now, after overnight trains took me from Irkutsk to Krasnoyarsk, from Krasnoyarsk to Yekaterinburg, from Yekaterinburg to Kazan, and now, from Kazan to Moscow. While I appreciated the efficiency of traveling overnight, the lack of sleep and the quandary of arriving early in a new city with no place to go was getting old.

Russian hostels were also getting old. They were not proving to be a place to make new travel friends, as everyone promised before my trip. Along the Trans-Siberian, they were largely empty apartments where I occupied the only bunk. When there were other guests, they stayed to themselves. Any hopes I had for making friends in my new Moscow hostel were diminished as soon as I arrived. With no empty bunk for me so early in the morning, a gruff young man who seemed to work there directed me to an attic-like space on the second floor of the hostel. With low, sloping ceilings and blue and brown cushions covering the floor, I felt like I was intruding on someone's secret make-out space. I laid down cautiously, using my shoulder bag as a pillow rather than lay my head on one of the dirty cushions, and tried to sleep.

A few hours later, I was sitting on the bottom bunk in a four-person dorm room with my laptop perched precariously on my knees. A whoosh of plastic hitting my shoulder broke my concentration. I looked up to see the three Russian girls who shared my room strutting out, their laughs echoing behind them. An empty Sprite bottle sat on the bed next to me. It landed far from their bunks or any waste basket, so I immediately assumed I was the target—a reaction that felt natural after a lifetime of being laughed at behind my back. To my relief, they hadn't returned by the time I went to bed. But in an encore of my first Moscow hostel experience, I lay awake for hours listening to drunken shrieks and breaking glass from the common area just steps from my room. Suddenly, I couldn't wait to board my overnight train to Latvia.

PART TWO
December-May

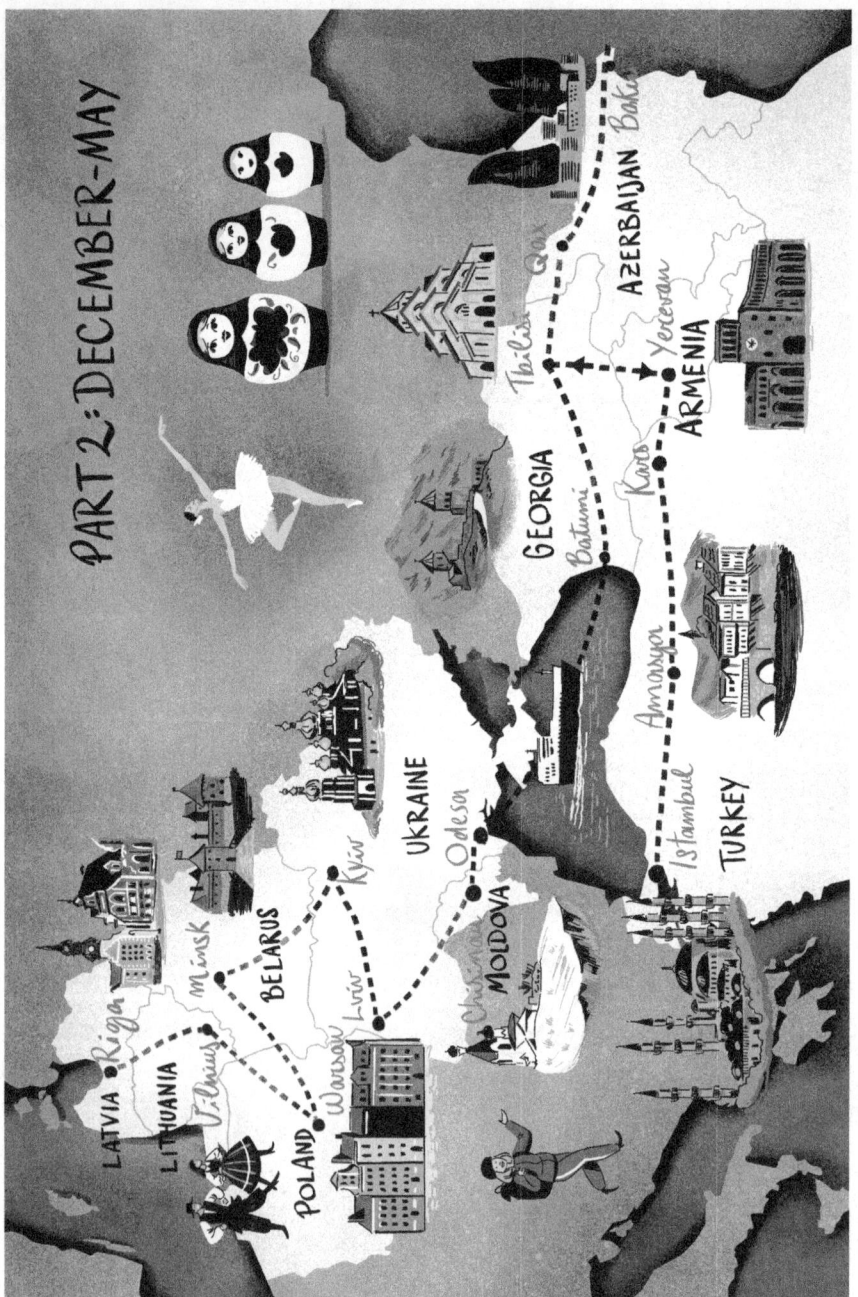

4
Latvia & Lithuania

I squinted as I stepped into the train station in Riga, the capital of Latvia. After a night on the train from Moscow, my eyes had to adjust to the bright station lights. It was a stark contrast to the dark, cold stations I'd encountered throughout Russia. I was relieved to see a large sign in English directing me to the tourist information booth, where I picked up a neatly folded map of the city. Just outside, I asked a woman for directions in English, and when she didn't know the answer, she asked another woman in Latvian, who responded in Russian. At that point, the first woman translated back to me in English, not realizing I could understand much of her Russian. They were both eager to help and full of smiles. I couldn't help but smile back.

My introduction to the Baltic states—Estonia, Latvia and Lithuania—had come three months earlier when I arrived in Tallinn, Estonia on a ferry from Helsinki. Because of the uncertainties around applying for my Russian visa, it made sense logistically to spend time in Estonia before moving on to St. Petersburg. I quickly fell in love with Tallinn's charm, from the cobblestone streets and outdoor cafes of the walled Old Town to its coastal setting on the Gulf of Finland. I managed to get lost at almost every turn, but that somehow only added to Tallinn's appeal. Arriving in Riga, I immediately felt like I was back in Tallinn.

After leaving the train station, I got on a trolley bus going in the wrong direction, and the driver kindly explained to me—in English—where I needed to go to catch the right one. I quickly realized that, just as in Tallinn, English was widely spoken in Riga, from the trolley bus driver to the hotel receptionist, to the cashier at the opera house. Once on the correct trolley, I was ecstatic when I saw not only a digital sign with the name of the approaching stop scrolling across the front of the bus but a TV screen showing all upcoming stops as well. In Russia, I felt lucky when I boarded a bus that had a conductor announcing the next stop. More typical were crowded marshrutkas where I had to watch carefully for my stop, call it out and hope the driver heard me.

In Riga, people crossed the street at crosswalks with stoplights, not through underground walkways that doubled as shopping centers, which was the norm in Moscow and St. Petersburg. The main department store in central Riga featured shelves lined with Schär gluten-free bread, cookies, and pasta. I had more to choose from than I did back home in Chicago. After three months of struggling to find food safe to eat, I was in heaven. While the sun set horribly early—around 3:30 p.m. since it was early December—the mild climate was a welcome relief from the snow and cold I'd endured in Siberia over the previous month. As I settled into my hostel in the center of the city, I suddenly realized how much Russia had challenged me. Riga felt easy by comparison.

Latvia and the Baltic states provided a historical contrast with Russia as well. Once officially Soviet states, it didn't take me long to realize that the Baltics never really considered themselves "Soviet." They didn't think they were part of the Soviet Union; they were occupied by it. My visit to the Museum of Occupation in Tallinn months earlier had made that clear. Indeed, all three Baltic countries had once been part of the Polish-Lithuanian Commonwealth, while Estonia and Latvia had also been under Swedish influence for decades before being conquered by Russia and then eventually subsumed into the Soviet Union. Upon gaining their independence in 1991, they increasingly looked to the West. By the time I visited in 2011, they had been members of both NATO and the European Union for seven years.

* * *

As I approached Arena Riga, the home of Dinamo Riga, the city's professional hockey team, I wondered if it would feel the same as a game back home. I'd only been to one professional hockey game in my life, but I grew up going to high school hockey games in Minnesota, and I'd been to countless professional basketball, football, and baseball games. After my parents divorced, my brother and I spent every other weekend at my dad's place. If we didn't spend Saturday afternoons playing catch, we were under the bubble of the Metrodome watching Minnesota Twins baseball. And if we weren't doing that, my brother and I sprawled out on the couch as my dad lounged in his recliner, watching whatever sport happened to be on television. My dad played college basketball and football, so it was only natural for him to pass that on to my brother and me. And frankly, I'm not sure he knew what else to do with us.

That interest in—and eventually, passion for—sports also provided an outlet for me to try to fit in. I started playing softball in elementary school and continued through junior high. While it gave me an ostensible group of friends, I always found myself on a losing team—something that drove the competitive side of me crazy. I often lamented to my dad that the "cool girls" were all on the winning teams. I picked up volleyball in junior high and persisted throughout high school, making the varsity team in my junior and senior years. Playing sports didn't endear me to the "in" crowd, but it provided opportunities to make new friends and helped me gain some much-needed confidence. Of course, Minnesota is the state of hockey, and more than football or basketball, hockey was the sport that excited people. I couldn't visit a former Soviet state like Latvia without going to a hockey game.

My ticket cost eight Lats (about $16) for a seat in the second row of the upper level, directly behind the goal. Walking into the arena, I was surrounded by men decked out in hockey jerseys or Dinamo Riga scarves and women with cute fake tattoos with the team logo decorating their faces. The only thing that may have set it apart from a typical game back home was the number of women donning four-inch heels and miniskirts to go with those fake tattoos. Although I seemed to be the only person by myself, I didn't feel nearly as self-conscious as I would have attending a sporting event—or any other event—solo at home. I was discovering one of the joys of solo travel. No one there knew me, so there was no one to judge me. And even if they did, what did I care?

The game was an early season match-up between two mediocre teams in the Kontinental Hockey League, yet it had a playoff atmosphere. Several men in the lower level banged on drums continuously, leading the rest of the arena in nonstop chants.

"Dee-na-MO! Dee-na-MO!"

During timeouts and intermissions, fans rushed to the restrooms and concession stands just as they would at home. The kiss cam ran on the Jumbotron, as did a feature that probably wouldn't fly in American arenas—placing the heads of random men in the crowd on top of an image of some very large cleavage. There were giveaways and even a marriage proposal. Despite the home team losing 5–2, the crowd's spirit never diminished. Unlike American crowds that infamously leave early to beat the traffic, the arena was still full when the final buzzer sounded. As fans filed out, they were still chanting and singing as if they'd won. I admired their passion—or their drunkenness.

As I walked back to my hostel, I was thankful that I decided to push myself outside my comfort zone to go to the game in the first place—something that I likely would not have done if I had been anywhere in the United States. At the same time, it was the most at ease I'd felt since leaving Chicago.

* * *

After a week in Riga, I moved on to Vilnius, the capital of Lithuania, and just a four-hour bus ride away. The days were getting shorter, so my time to explore each day was limited. My main goal in Vilnius was to get my visa to Belarus, the first visa I would try to obtain on the road. I'd acquired my Russian visa while I was still in Chicago, anxiously dropping my brand-new passport off at the post office and then counting the days until it came back with a full-page visa sticker stuck neatly on the first page. While I'd traveled to more than a dozen countries before this trip, I'd never had to apply for a visa in advance. The fact that many former Soviet countries required entry visas added an extra layer of complexity as I tried to plan my itinerary. It explained why I had to stop in Lithuania before going to Belarus and why, eventually, I would spend a week in Azerbaijan trying to get visas to Tajikistan and Uzbekistan and then a week in Tashkent as I waited on my Kazakhstan visa.

For now, I only needed a visa to Belarus. While I waited the necessary week for my paperwork to be processed, I experimented with working with a tourism board for the first time. My travel blog was just over a year old, and the idea of making a living as a travel blogger intrigued me. As I contemplated leaving my first career as a tax attorney years earlier, I took an online travel agent training course, but I never found the confidence to take the next step of launching a travel business. The extent of my travels at that point had been a few group trips to Europe, a handful of solo trips to "easy" destinations like Australia, and an ill-fated trip to Peru with a high school friend who stopped speaking to me afterward. I convinced myself I wasn't qualified to plan trips for other people. I also wasn't ready to try something I wasn't confident I could succeed at, so I pushed dreams of a travel business aside. When I ultimately quit my tax lawyer job, I opted for a relatively secure career in higher education fundraising.

As I found myself at a professional crossroads once again, the idea of a career in travel persisted. In the year and a half that I spent preparing for this trip, I had discovered the world of travel blogs and social media. Long before Instagram influencers and TikTok stars, people started blogs to share their travel experiences and inspire others. Eventually, a few of the most ambitious bloggers found ways to monetize their websites. A few months before departing, I even went to a conference for aspiring travel bloggers in Vancouver, Canada. Some were using their blogs as platforms to get paid travel writing assignments and brand sponsorships, while others simply hoped for some free hotel stays in exchange for a blog post and a few tweets. It seemed like a good way to fund a travel lifestyle and this trip presented the perfect opportunity to try it out.

The Vilnius Tourism Board was the first tourism board to say yes when I reached out about working together. They offered me a two-night stay at a hotel near one of the main city gates, as well as a multi-day pass to the major attractions in the Old Town. Wanting to make the most of the opportunity and to build a portfolio of work, I threw myself into exploring every block of Vilnius as I waited for my Belarusian visa.

I started with an audio guided tour of the Old Town. The guide led me through more than 90 stops, including monuments, memorials, significant streets, churches, and museums. Standing at one end of Stikliu Street, I heard about the history of the Jewish ghetto in Vilnius. As I walked down Bostko Street, the guide filled me in on the legend of the founding of the city. According to the legend, the Grand Duke of Lithuania, Gediminas, fell asleep in the woods after a day of hunting. He dreamed that a large iron wolf was standing on top of a hill, with hundreds of other wolves howling all around it. A pagan priest interpreted the dream to mean that a castle and town should be built on that spot, and the town would become the capital of Lithuania. Indeed, the city of Vilnius was built around what is now called Gediminas Hill, which I climbed to the top of for a sweeping view of the entire city. I probably learned more about Vilnius and Lithuanian history in one day than I did in a month in Moscow or St. Petersburg.

In Cathedral Square, I listened to the story behind the "Stebuklas" tile, which marked the end of the 650-kilometer human chain that was formed between Tallinn, Riga, and Vilnius on August 23, 1989, to protest the Soviet occupation of the Baltic states. The word *stebuklas* means "miracle" in Lithuanian. Approximately two million people joined hands to form the human chain that covered 370 miles—kind of like forming a chain from Chicago to Minneapolis. It was hard for me to fathom, but it was symbolic of the anti-Soviet sentiment and the burning desire for freedom throughout the Baltics.

Another day, I visited the Museum of Genocide Victims, which was in a building that served as the KGB (Soviet secret police) headquarters for almost 50 years. It also served as a memorial to those killed by the KGB, and their names were inscribed on the exterior of the building. Exhibits in 10 rooms over two floors displayed historical material from 1940 to 1991, detailing the loss of Lithuanian independence, its occupation by both Nazi Germany and the Soviet Union, and its fight to regain its independence in the early 1990s. In the basement was the former KGB prison, left as it was when the KGB moved out in 1991. I realized that, despite majoring in Russian and East European Studies in college, I had a lot to learn about Soviet history. So much had been glossed over in my classes, I was starting to wonder if I had really learned anything at all.

With 10 days to kill in Vilnius, I also took several day trips outside the city, the highlight of which was the Hill of Crosses in Siauliai, three hours away. Visiting an ostensible religious site was an admittedly odd choice for someone who isn't religious. Nearly all my memories from church growing up were negative. The Baptist church my parents sent us to as kids was cold and insular—and provided no respite from the teasing I endured at school. Even my Sunday School teacher joined in, reciting a jingle about London, France and my underpants while no one else was paying attention. Even after we changed congregations in junior high, the hypocrisy and judgment of the church cast a constant shadow. I hated the pressure to try to bring friends to convert—they even wanted to turn my Catholic best friend into a Baptist. Although I was just a teenager, I already believed that no religion was better or more "correct" than another. I also naively thought that church should be a place where I could be accepted for who I was. I was clearly wrong.

Despite my apprehension about organized religion, when traveling, I recognized how much religion, culture, and history could be intertwined. When I visited the Church of Our Saviour on Spilled Blood in St. Petersburg and the Ivolginsky Datsan outside of Ulan Ude, I chose to focus on the historical and aesthetic aspects over the religious. The same was true for the Hill of Crosses. While the origins of the Hill may have been religious in nature—Lithuania historically is a Catholic country—it evolved to become a place for Lithuanians to pray for their country and to remember loved ones who passed away. After the Soviets invaded in 1944, it also became a symbol of resistance. The Soviets tried to bulldoze the site multiple times, but the Hill of Crosses endured.

With more than 100,000 crosses spread out around a large mound in all directions, the Hill was a fascinating site to explore. I spent several hours inspecting crosses in all shapes and sizes, made of wood, metal, or plastic. Smaller crosses dangled on rosaries hung on larger crosses. Many included names and dates, often memorializing family members. The sheer volume of crosses was overwhelming. I didn't need to be religious to be moved by the collective hope and sorrow they represented, both individually and for an entire country. Perhaps it was the overcast skies or the heaviness of the crosses surrounding me, but I left with a feeling of melancholy that I hadn't felt in a long time. That feeling was only exacerbated by what happened next.

* * *

I stared at my laptop, anxiously awaiting the familiar tone

of a Skype call coming in. My friends were gathered in Chicago for our annual holiday cookie-baking party, and they planned to call me. I hadn't talked to any of them since my going away party four months earlier. Email exchanges had become sporadic. No one had even responded to the update I'd sent a couple weeks earlier. Many of them didn't understand why this trip meant so much to me, and my pleas to hear about their lives were met with, "You don't want to hear about what I'm doing; it's boring compared to you." That could not have been further from the truth. Even though I was half a world away, I really wanted to hear about the bad dates, the drunken nights out, and the evil bosses. I didn't want to feel like I was missing as much as I was.

As the minutes passed without a call, I began to wonder if they had forgotten. Five minutes turned into 10 minutes, which turned into half an hour. I pulled up my friend Laura's email to make sure I had the time right—I did—and then sent off a note asking if we were still on. By the time an hour had passed, I had to admit my friends had forgotten about me. I closed my laptop and lay back on the pristine bed in my spotless hotel room in Vilnius and started to cry.

My quiet tears soon turned into uncontrollable sobbing. I was devastated. Other long-term travelers warned me this would happen, but it still broke my heart to feel like such a chasm had grown between my friends and me. It was also hard for me to admit I was struggling—even to myself. Before I left, my dad made me promise that if I wasn't enjoying the trip, I would come home. He reminded me of my freshman year of college at Iowa. While my high school friends were all making new friends, going to parties, and generally loving college, I was dealing with one roommate who struggled with mental health issues and another who was a promiscuous drunk. I was missing a boy back home, and my goody-two-shoes nature and tendency to follow the rules made it challenging to make new friends in my dorm, where drinking seemed to be the only way to socialize. Rather than share my difficulties with anyone, I put up a façade and pretended all was okay.

This trip was no different. I felt like most people saw it as an extended vacation where I would be having a blast every day. Whenever anyone asked how it was going, they expected only an upbeat reply. While I figured I would face challenges, I had to admit the first few months were more difficult than I'd anticipated, from the disappointing homestays and volunteer experiences to my inability to connect with many like-minded travelers. I'd worked for more than a year to make this trip a reality. I quit a good job, stopped pursuing romantic relationships, drifted from friends, and sold everything I owned. I researched and read for hours about all the places I wanted to visit. I drafted one itinerary after another and created detailed spreadsheets to develop a budget and track my spending. But I never really stopped to think about how it would be. How would it feel to be on the road, traveling on my own, for months on end?

As I lay in my hotel room in Vilnius, I kept thinking how it sometimes didn't feel real. I wondered, "Is this really me? Is this really my life?" At times it felt like I was on the outside sneaking a peek at someone else's life. As I'd prepared to board the flight to Helsinki months earlier, I kept waiting to experience some deep epiphany about what I was about to do, but never happened. It occurred to me that I may have taken it all for granted. As I launched my travel blog, joined the travel blogging community and befriended so many others who were traveling full-time, I almost forgot that it wasn't normal. I couldn't appreciate the uniqueness of my experience, and I had a hard time giving myself credit for what I accomplished in my first three months on the road. Instead, I looked at my friends back home and saw engagements, marriages, pregnancies, and job promotions. And I looked back at myself and felt like I was being left behind.

At the same time, I felt like I wasn't living up to the expectations of my new travel friends or myself. While the travel bloggers I met online headed to backpacker-friendly destinations like Thailand, Laos, and Vietnam, I'd made things harder for myself by choosing a more challenging route through the former Soviet states. Those friends shared stories of going out every night, meeting new people, and hooking up with multiple guys. While that had never been my style, part of me wished it was.

I knew in my heart that was not what my trip was about. I could've spent my days river tubing in Vang Vieng or beach hopping in Phuket. But I had to stay true to myself. From the very beginning, I saw a more serious purpose for my trip—to discover a direction for my life and a path for my future. I'd been expecting a magic moment to happen when the light bulb would go on, and I'd think, "Yes, it all makes sense now. This is what I want to do. This is what I'm meant to do." After three months on the road, I was beginning to wonder if that moment would ever come.

5
Warsaw

The moon was still high in the night sky as I stepped off the overnight bus from Vilnius shortly after 5 a.m. The other passengers quickly scattered in all directions, leaving me alone outside of Warsaw's main bus station. I didn't feel comfortable wandering around the city in the dark, trying to find my hotel. I couldn't justify splurging on a taxi. I found an empty bench inside the station to call home for the next couple of hours. I shivered as I tried to focus on reading my Kindle, my sleepless eyes occasionally falling shut for seconds, even minutes, at a time. The late-December cold and fatigue finally wore me down. By 7 a.m., I figured enough people would be out on the streets of Warsaw to make me feel safe walking to the hotel despite the lingering darkness.

While Poland was not part of the former Soviet Union, it was certainly within the sphere of Soviet influence. Indeed, I wrote a report for a high school history class about the Warsaw Pact, a collective defense treaty between the Soviet Union, Poland, and several other Eastern and Central European countries. It also made a good side trip. My date for entering Belarus was fixed for early January, so I needed someplace to spend the holidays. I initially planned to stop in Warsaw on my way to Krakow, where I would ring in 2012. I fondly recalled bringing in 2009 in Prague's Old Town Square among thousands of people counting down to the new year as fireworks went off at midnight. I imagined Krakow having a similar atmosphere. I even thought I could convince a friend or two from home to fly over to join me, but no one would. Then, in early December, I learned that the traditional celebration on the square in Krakow had been canceled. According to the hostel I'd booked, clubbing was the most likely alternative. Not wanting a repeat of my Moscow nightclub experience and petrified of the idea of going to a club on New Year's Eve by myself, I opted to stay in Warsaw.

Luck was with me when I arrived at my hotel just blocks from the train station. My room was ready and I quickly burrowed under the covers for a much-needed nap. When I awoke, I opened my email to discover an electronic Christmas card sent by Laura. As I scrolled through the names of dozens of friends who had signed it, I was in awe of how many people Laura managed to include. Not only were there notes from our close circle of friends, but there were messages from college friends, law school friends and even new friends from the improv class I took just before I left. I wasn't sure how many Laura even knew personally. While many of the notes were nothing more than "Merry Christmas," feelings of gratitude and humility replaced the hurt from the missed Skype call in Vilnius. Maybe my friends hadn't completely forgotten about me after all. And even though most didn't understand why I had left Chicago to travel the world, perhaps they supported my decision more than I realized.

Later that evening, I logged on for another Skype call, this time to celebrate Christmas with my family back in Minnesota. This was the first Christmas I'd ever missed, but I struggled to feel nostalgic about it. Christmas was never a happy time of year for me. From the time I threw up all over the dinner table as a three-year-old to the time someone stole all our Christmas presents from our car on Christmas Eve, the holiday didn't generate good memories. Perhaps it was the stress of bouncing among obligatory gatherings with extended family that felt impersonal and rushed. Or it may have been the compulsory time spent with the stepfather I couldn't stand and the way he encroached upon the Christmas morning traditions my brother and I had created. Or maybe it was the emphasis on the religious aspect of the holiday, a piece I wasn't sure I ever believed in. While I'm sure my family missed me, I was almost relieved to escape all the usual madness.

But I did look forward to seeing my niece over Skype. She was just approaching her second birthday, and I wondered if she would recognize me through a computer screen. With no kids of my own and no desire to have any, I'd decided to throw myself into being the best, coolest aunt I could be. More than anything, I wanted to instill in my niece a love of travel that my brother and his wife didn't share. So, from my small hotel room in Warsaw, I called them on Christmas and watched on a tiny screen as my niece and others opened their presents from each other and from me; I'd managed to send home a box from Russia with a few carefully selected gifts, like the nesting doll set painted as the Minnesota Vikings that I so proudly bartered for in Moscow.

After splurging on a hotel for Christmas, I moved to a hostel in Warsaw's Stare Miasto (Old Town), hoping to meet some fellow travelers with whom I could ring in the new year. With a week to explore, I spent hours wandering along the cobblestone streets of Stare Miasto and Nowe Miasto (New Town). Buildings painted in yellow, green, and orange looked like they hailed from the 19th century, not the mid-20th century. The Royal Castle, left with just one wall standing in 1944, dominated Plac Zamkowy and, during my visit, served as an attractive backdrop for a large Christmas tree on the square. Heading out from the Old Town, streets like Krakowskie Przedmieście and Nowy Świat had a quaint charm that I didn't often find in large cities. Perhaps it was just the festive Christmas lights that adorned the lamp posts and building fronts, but I found this stretch of Warsaw's Old Royal Road more attractive than counterparts like the Champs-Élysées in Paris, Nevsky Prospekt in St. Petersburg, or Las Ramblas in Barcelona.

At the same time, I wasn't prepared for what I would learn about the city's tragic history. As a few different Couchsurfers showed me around, I heard a common refrain: "That was destroyed in the war." We walked past markers where walls of the Jewish ghetto once stood—the ghetto created by the Nazis that imprisoned 380,000 Jews in an area covering 18 kilometers. A monument on Stawki Street showed where the Nazis loaded over 300,000 Jews into cattle wagons to transport them to the gas chambers at Treblinka, 100 kilometers northwest of Warsaw. Additional markers led to a monument honoring those who fought in the Ghetto Uprising of 1943. By the time the Nazis quashed the uprising, the former Jewish quarter in Warsaw basically no longer existed. Outside the Jewish Cemetery, a memorial stood where two mass graves were discovered, filled with bones of men and women from a retirement home who had been brought to the spot only to be shot and killed. The cemetery itself held over 250,000 graves, many marked by intricately carved gravestones now covered in bright green moss and dull brown leaves.

Although I learned about World War II and the Holocaust in both high school and college, the stark reality of what happened never really sunk in. We studied dates and numbers and politics, with little emphasis on the tragic human realities. Visiting Warsaw made it all seem more real. I spent hours at the Warsaw Uprising Museum, which chronicled life during the Nazi occupation, the daily events of the 1944 Uprising, and the aftermath. I listened to interviews with survivors who fought for their city and their country. I watched film footage from the first month of the uprising. I saw photographs of the city after the Nazis tried to bomb it out of existence. I visited the Pawiak Prison, where the Nazis executed nearly 40,000 prisoners and gathered another 60,000 to take to extermination camps. I listened to a survivor, a man who'd been imprisoned when he was only 15. He told us that the worst part wasn't the beatings (they could expect the beatings), but rather listening to the screams of fellow imprisoned people as they were beaten.

While Warsaw's lowest points were during World War II, the Soviet occupation brought Stalinist terror and decades of communist rule. Across the street from the U.S. Embassy, a statue of former U.S. President Ronald Reagan portrayed him standing at a podium in front of Berlin's Brandenburg Gate in 1987 when he declared, "Mr. Gorbachev, tear down this wall." I was just 11 when I watched that moment on television, not fully understanding what it meant at the time. As I stopped in front of the statue, a man close to my parents' age spoke to me emotionally about Reagan's role in ending the Cold War and "freeing Poland from Russia." By the end of a week of immersing myself in Warsaw's past, I had a somber feeling about the city and an appreciation for the fact I was even there. My dilemma over how to celebrate New Year's Eve seemed petty in comparison.

* * *

My hostel was eerily quiet when I returned from an afternoon of exploring the day before New Year's Eve. I hadn't succeeded in making friends with the few other guests I encountered, but most seemed to be gone anyway. As I prepared dinner for myself alone in the small kitchen, memories of past New Year's Eves floated in my head. I felt weighed down both by the gravity of everything I'd learned in Warsaw and by my self-imposed pressure to do something cool to ring in 2012. The next day, I retreated to a hotel on Nowy Swiat to do what I'd never done before: spend New Year's Eve alone.

Throughout my 20s and early 30s, New Year's Eve

seemed to be the one night of the year that I absolutely could not stay home, no matter how much I wanted to. But from a spiked drink at a hotel party to overcrowded bars to ill-advised hook-ups to pounding hangovers, it never lived up to expectations. How many times did I go out hoping to get that perfect midnight kiss only to find myself standing on the sidelines alone, watching everyone else belting out "Auld Lang Syne?" How many times did I reluctantly embrace a guy I couldn't care less about just because he was there while I secretly longed for someone else? How many times did I wake up on New Year's Day just feeling miserable—physically and emotionally?

So I enjoyed an early dinner out and then crawled into bed with CNN International on the television and my laptop perched on my knees. I could see the drizzle outside my window turn into a steady freezing rain, reinforcing my decision to stay in. Hours later, as fireworks exploded above the square just a few blocks away, I looked inward. While I reflected upon my four months of travel, I tried to look ahead and make resolutions for the coming year. I decided to get a head start by cleaning out my social media contacts, unfriending and unfollowing those who no longer provided value in my life. As I scrolled through my Facebook friends list, one name kept jumping out at me: Patrick.

I smiled as I recalled meeting the red-faced guy with spiky blond hair and a mischievous smile for the first time more than four years earlier. His warm eyes connected with mine as we bonded over stories of traveling around Europe half-drunk when we were in our early twenties. When I asked where else he wanted to go, Russia was the first country that rolled off his lips. He was one of more than a dozen strangers I was about to join for a week-long ski trip in Saalbach, Austria. I couldn't contain my excitement when I called my best friend Krina on my way home from the bar two hours later.

"I just met the most amazing guy," I gushed. "This ski trip is going to be awesome. I can't wait!"

I saw Patrick again a week later at Chicago O'Hare as our group gathered to catch our flight to Munich, and our conversation picked up where we'd left off. By the end of our first night in Saalbach, we were kissing at the bar. Our first "date" came two days later as the group took a day trip to Salzburg. Patrick and I spent the day exploring the city best known for the *Sound of Music,* and I fell asleep on his shoulder on the bus back to Saalbach that evening. We spent what was meant to be our last day on the slopes snuggling in my twin-size bed, recovering from hangovers from the night before. As he kissed my forehead before we fell asleep in each other's arms, I was smitten.

The initial awkwardness of our first date back in Chicago morphed into the easiness of lounging in bed quizzing each other on professional sports team names. He called me at work to surprise me with tickets to the Big Ten basketball tournament, and I invited him to join me for celebratory drinks when I quit my job as a lawyer to take a job fundraising for a local law school. He joined my March Madness basketball pool and met up with my friends for happy hour. Krina jokingly warned him he better not break my heart while his friend Sarah ominously suggested to me that he may not be over an ex-girlfriend. When he bought us tickets to see the Killers two months down the road, I took it as a sign we were a couple.

But just a week after driving home in silence from the Killers concert, I sat on my couch, trying to hold back tears. I stared into his eyes, searching for the connection I'd felt so strongly the night we'd met. He looked away as he said the words I was dreading.

"I can't…I just can't," he repeated. "I'm sorry. I know it's not fair."

He went on to tell me he didn't want to hurt our "friendship," but in my mind, it was too late for that. I was in love; I didn't want to be just friends. I was tired of being friends. Scott, Dean, Brandon, Brad, Matt, Joe. They all wanted to be just friends. I thought, for the first time, that Patrick would be different.

As soon as he left, the tears started flowing, and they didn't stop for days. I'd ride the bus downtown to work and start crying. I sat in my new office looking out on Jackson Boulevard and struggled to get through each day. I wasn't just sad about Patrick. I was sad about every guy who came before him. I had felt a stronger and more immediate connection with him than any guy I'd ever known, yet I couldn't make it work, so how would I ever make it work with anyone? I blamed myself for pushing too hard, for not giving him enough space—but more than anything, for not being enough. I wasn't pretty enough. I wasn't smart enough. I wasn't funny enough. I wasn't sexy enough. Whatever it was that guys wanted, I clearly wasn't enough of it. When I met Patrick, I was so convinced that he was the one that when it ended, all I could do was believe that I was just meant to be single forever.

As the one-year anniversary of the ski trip and meeting Patrick approached, I decided I needed to be doing something amazing while he was off skiing again with many of our mutual friends. The last thing I wanted was to be sitting at home wondering what he was doing. So I booked a trip to Egypt. Not only did Egypt keep me from thinking about Patrick, but it also exposed me to traveling off the beaten path and in a less-developed part of the world for the first time. As I crawled inside of pyramids and explored ruins of ancient cities, my love of travel grew deeper. Just as Russia became an obsession when I was an insecure teenager, travel became my passion as a broken-hearted 31-year-old. My escape to Egypt set the stage for me to eventually quit my job to travel the world.

But now, as I stared at Patrick's smiling face on my computer screen, I knew it was time to truly move on. My cursor hovered above his name, and I quickly clicked "unfriend" before I could change my mind. While I probably wouldn't have been ringing in the new year in a Warsaw hotel room but for him, I knew I couldn't continue my journey of self-discovery with memories of him weighing me down. I needed to let him go for good.

6
Belarus

I stepped into the bathroom stall at the National Opera and Ballet Theatre in Minsk and gasped in shock. I was standing in front of the nicest, cleanest squat toilet I'd ever seen. I'd encountered plenty of these when I visited Egypt a few years earlier. I was mildly surprised when I saw one at the train station in Veliky Novgorod, Russia, but I came to expect them as I traveled throughout Siberia. I never imagined that I would encounter a squat toilet in the shiny new opera house in the capital of Belarus. I could only imagine the challenge facing the women waiting in line behind me: crouching in four-inch heels while holding their sequined gowns or taffeta skirts out of the way. Of course, as I was wearing my fanciest travel outfit of black pants and ballet flats, I had no issues.

Originally opened in 1939, the opera house had been extensively renovated in recent years. The white marble corridors featured gold accents and glittering chandeliers. Inside the theater, gold trim adorned the walls and red velvet seats. It felt far more luxurious than the historic Mariinsky Theater I'd visited in St. Petersburg, but the ticket price did not reflect that. I purchased my ticket for the Russian opera, *Snegurochka*, online for 28,000 rubles, the equivalent of just $3. I bought a program for a few cents and was pleased to find English translations explaining each act. That was far more than I got when I went to the opera in Rome years earlier.

Of the countries I'd visited so far, I probably knew the least about Belarus. I added it to my itinerary solely because of its status as a former Soviet state. Russia had been my original target when I decided I wanted to take a career break to travel. Still reeling from my breakup with Patrick and feeling increasingly out of place in my life in Chicago, I thought I would quit my job in the spring and spend the summer traveling through Russia. I would relocate to Minnesota with a new job in the fall. But after being offered a promotion at work—one too good to pass up—I decided to delay the trip by a year. I figured it would be better for my resume and my bank account, but it also gave me time to dream bigger.

I started reading about the Silk Road and became intrigued by the 'Stans of Central Asia. The Baltic states had been on my radar since I wrote a journal article about them in law school. Georgia and Armenia sounded fascinating as well. At some point, I decided to look up a list of every country that had been part of the Soviet Union. I thrive on having goals to pursue, so when I saw that there were 15 former Soviet states, I thought it would be a worthwhile goal to visit all of them.

With Belarus, I was excited and intrigued to visit a place that most Americans didn't even have on their radar, but I worried about it more than any country I had visited to date. I was concerned about the language barrier, which was silly because I made it through Russia for three months just fine. I fretted about getting around, which was even sillier because the metro in Minsk was about one-tenth the size of Moscow's. But mostly, I was anxious because I imagined Belarus would be sort of like Russia, but worse—poorer, less modern, less stable, and less free. Russia had been a struggle for me, and I feared Belarus could be even more of a challenge.

I couldn't have been more wrong.

* * *

"You're late."

A woman with auburn hair and a dark pink beret stood in front of me with a smile, shaking her head.

"I am?" I replied, wrinkling my eyebrows in confusion. According to my Blackberry, I had arrived in Minsk a few minutes early. But a glance at the clock on the wall of the central bus station confirmed that the woman greeting me was correct. It was an hour later than I thought it was. Only later did I realize that, like Russia, Belarus eliminated the concept of daylight savings time. When everyone else in Europe turned their clocks back in the fall, the time in Belarus remained the same. My Blackberry didn't recognize the difference.

To reach Minsk, I'd backtracked from Warsaw to Vilnius on an overnight bus and then departed Vilnius on an early morning bus for Minsk. The border crossing was surprisingly painless. Unlike when I entered Russia, we didn't have to leave the bus at the border—no questioning at an immigration window, no declaring anything at customs, and no walking through metal detectors. I just handed over my passport with my Belarusian visa pasted inside and showed a copy of the mandatory medical insurance I purchased for $10 in Vilnius. An officer quickly stamped me through.

The newly renovated bus station was impressive, with numbered platforms and digital signs displaying upcoming departure times. Next door, a multi-level train station was clean, bright, and warm, looking and feeling much nicer than anything I had seen in Moscow or St. Petersburg. The woman waiting for me as I stepped off the bus was Yuliya. We'd met in Vilnius, where I'd switched from my hotel to a hostel as I waited for my visa to Belarus to be processed. Although we shared a dorm room for three days, we only crossed paths as Yuliya prepared to depart. A five-minute conversation led to her offering to meet me and show me around Minsk. I took the offer with a grain of salt, not really expecting a total stranger to give up her time to show me around her city. But three weeks and several emails later, here she was.

After gathering my bags, our first stop was the currency exchange inside the neighboring train station. While the exchange rate listed in my 2008 guidebook was 3,045 Belarusian rubles to the dollar, by early 2012, the rate was 8,450 to the dollar. I changed my 20 Polish zlotych for 48,340 Belarusian rubles and 50 euros for 530,000 rubles. Within 15 minutes of arriving, I had bills totaling almost 600,000 in my wallet. They were worth less than $70.

Yuliya and I then caught the metro to drop my bags at

my hotel before meeting her husband, Andrei, for lunch. Hostels hadn't really arrived in Belarus yet, and I had to make a hotel reservation through a local tour company to obtain the letter of invitation necessary for my visa. This was a concept that carried over from Soviet times; many former Soviet states, including Russia, required visitors to submit a letter from a hotel or tour company providing the basis for their visit. The letters varied in their legitimacy. To obtain the visa I needed to stay in Russia for three months, I paid a visa company based in London to issue me a letter stating I was visiting Russia for some sort of business purpose. For Belarus, I simply worked with a local tour company to make all my hotel arrangements, and they were happy to give me the letter I needed.

The metro in Minsk was simple yet confusing. There were only two lines, and they crossed in the center—just a fraction of the size of Moscow's system and without the five-minute escalator rides up and down. To ride, I bought a purple plastic token (a *zheton*), which cost 1,300 rubles (about 15 cents). It looked like a piece from a children's board game. Most signs in the station were in Belarusian. Announcements were made primarily in Belarusian, with the occasional secondary message in Russian. However, some of the stops had Russian and Belarusian names that were quite different from each other. For example, the metro lines crossed at the Kupalovskaya and Oktyabrskaya stations, but the conductor and the map I got from my hotel both referred to Oktyabrskaya as Kastrichnitskaya. Similarly, later in the week, Yuliya told me to meet her at the Vostok stop, which was called Ushod on the official map.

Over the next four days, Yuliya and Andrei gave me a glimpse into their lives as 30-something Belarusians. In many ways, they had a lot in common with me and my friends: working office jobs and spending their free time going out with friends. On the other hand, Yuliya told me how her grandmother longed for Soviet days because the government provided for everyone then. There hadn't been such a gap between rich and poor. This divide was evident as we drove outside of Minsk. The suburbs were lined with large brick houses that you might expect to find on the North Shore of Chicago. Yuliya explained that too many people cheated the system, leading to the rich getting richer and the poor getting poorer. According to her, the average salary was about $150 to $300 per month (shortly after I left, the government announced it would increase to $500 per month).

Over dinner one night, Yuliya shared that she believed she was free in many ways to do what she wanted; she could come and go as she pleased and travel out of the country, which was more than my guide Olga in Ulan Ude could do. Yuliya could even study at a university in another country, which is what she was doing when I met her in Vilnius. These were things that I took for granted; whether I had the freedom to travel overseas or study abroad was never a question for me. My only constraints were time and money.

I was surprised to see that the police presence in Minsk was minimal compared to Russia. Yuliya confirmed that police did not stop people randomly to check their "documents" as they often did in Moscow. While I was never stopped for a document check in Russia, the possibility was always in the back of my mind. The light police presence in Minsk oddly meant I felt more comfortable walking around there than I had in any major city in Russia.

But Yuliya also pointed out the lack of freedom in Belarus, particularly with respect to the lack of a free press and restrictions on expressing negative views about the government. Indeed, a guy in my Warsaw hostel warned me not to use my Blackberry near the central square in Minsk if any protests took place because the government would trace it and arrest me. When I purchased a Wi-Fi code at my Minsk hotel, they tracked it, giving me the distinct impression that my internet use may be monitored. Yuliya told me she didn't foresee democracy ever really taking hold in Belarus. She longed to leave the country for what she believed would be a better life elsewhere in Europe.

To my surprise, Andrei told me they didn't consider Belarus to be part of Europe; they simply saw themselves as part of the former Soviet Union. Perhaps most telling, as Yuliya and I spoke quietly in English while walking through a museum one afternoon, she said it was good we were talking in English because if anyone understood what we were discussing, they might take her away in handcuffs. She spoke with a smile, but I had to assume she was at least partly serious.

Our conversations intrigued me. It was one thing to read in my college textbooks about communism, Soviet times, and the fall of the Soviet Union. It was something else to be able to talk to people who had lived it all. I was in high school when the Soviet Union collapsed, not long after I first read about Catherine the Great. Between my fascination with Russia and history unfolding before my eyes, I was drawn to Russian and East European Studies as my college major in 1994. But as I traveled through these countries for the first time, I was reminded time and time again how much those college classes did not teach me. We memorized events and statistics and learned about political systems and theories. But we didn't learn about the people and the effects of such events and politics on their daily lives.

*   *   *

Yuliya played tour guide for me throughout my visit while Andrei was working. Perhaps it was because we were closer in age than Olya and I had been, but I developed a comfort level with her that had been missing when I explored Moscow with Olya. Yuliya accompanied me to an open-air folk museum, a museum about the Great Patriotic War, and a national culture and history museum. She also took me to the roof of the National Library at dusk for a sprawling view of the entire city.

Like Warsaw, Minsk was destroyed in World War II, so almost every building dated from the 1940s or later. For that reason, it seemed to lack the grit of some of the cities I visited in Russia. The sidewalks were wide and clean, many lined with brick rather than cement. Street signs stood out in bright blue and red. While many buildings had a distinctly Soviet feel to them, the main drag of the city was anything but unattractive. Several large squares, a few tree-covered parks, and a river running through the center prevented Minsk from feeling industrial or boring. A small "Old Town" area featured a couple churches and a hilly park overlooking the river, all of which were nicely illuminated at night. And there was the requisite Lenin statue and a few war monuments, including a memorial to those who died in the Soviet War in Afghanistan.

On the weekend, Yuliya and Andrei took me to see the must-see sights outside of the city: castles in the towns of Mir and Niasviž and the memorial site at Khatyn. While Mir and Niasviž were accessible by public transportation, it was more common for tourists to visit as part of an organized excursion. The only ways to reach Khatyn were by driving, joining a tour, or hiring a very expensive taxi. Despite the low cost of metro tokens and opera tickets, private tours and cars were as pricey as anywhere else. With my tight budget, I likely wouldn't have visited if Yuliya and Andrei hadn't insisted on taking me.

Neither Andrei nor Yuliya had ever been to Khatyn. Before we entered the memorial site, I pulled out my Kindle and started to read out loud from my guidebook. It described Khatyn as a once thriving community in a picturesque, wooded area where, in 1943, German troops encircled the village, drove everyone into a barn and barricaded the doors before dousing it in gasoline and setting it on fire. My voice cracked, and I tried to hide the tears welling in the corners of my eyes as I continued to describe the massacre that killed 149 people, including 75 children.

The grounds of the memorial site were laid out as the village of Khatyn once was. Twenty-six structures marked the locations of the 26 homes in the village that were burned to the ground, each consisting of a concrete foundation, a symbolic open gate, and an obelisk crowned with a bell. Plaques on the obelisks identified the deceased, listing the ages of any children. All the bells tolled together every 30 seconds, representing the rate at which citizens of Belarus were killed during World War II. On a gray day in January, with almost no one else at the site and surrounded by silence, the echoing sound sent shivers down my spine.

A symbolic cemetery served as a memorial for the other 185 villages in Belarus that the Nazis burned to the ground. Each village had a "grave" with its name, the name of the region where it was located, and an urn with soil from the village. Several "trees of life" featured the names of the 433 villages that were later rebuilt. Finally, an eternal flame memorialized the more than two million citizens of Belarus who were killed during World War II: one out of every four. Yet, just as with so much of the suffering in Warsaw that was glossed over in my history and political science classes, this chapter in Belarus' history was completely unknown to me. It was heartbreaking.

Glancing at Yuliya and Andrei as we explored the site, I could see that visiting Khatyn affected them as well. I couldn't imagine what they might be feeling as they experienced it for the first time, and I didn't have the words to ask them.

* * *

After five days under the care of Yuliya and Andrei, it was time for me to strike out on my own in Belarus. I was nervously excited for the challenge of navigating around the country without Yuliya as my guide, and I was curious to explore cities beyond Minsk. I made my way to the central bus station to catch a marshrutka to Grodno, a small city near the borders with Poland and Lithuania. A schedule was clearly posted at the station, but I ultimately didn't need it. A driver saw me staring at a vehicle labeled for Grodno, asked if I was going there, and then walked me to the cashier's office to buy my ticket. A three-and-a-half-hour express minivan cost me less than $10.

Grodno historically was part of the Grand Duchy of Lithuania and then the Polish-Lithuanian Commonwealth. The town wasn't pulled into the Russian Empire until the reign of Catherine the Great. It wasn't part of the Soviet Union until the start of World War II, when it was incorporated into the Belarusian Soviet Socialist Republic. It didn't surprise me, then, that Grodno didn't feel very Russian or very Soviet. The only evidence I saw of Soviet influence was the main square called Sovetskaya Square. Despite its precarious location, Grodno did not suffer severe damage during World War II. Many old buildings were still standing, including a 12th century church and a convent founded in 1642. There were no major sights to see in Grodno—just a few churches, a green, hilly park with a small river running through it, and an underwhelming museum. After a packed schedule of sightseeing in Minsk, I enjoyed just wandering around the town for two days at a relaxed pace, soaking in the cuteness.

As much as I adored Grodno, I was eager to move on to Brest, near the Polish border. Everything I read about it filled me with high expectations. Guidebooks described it as Western-influenced and cosmopolitan, yet calm, relaxed, and full of charm and grace. Yet when I exited the bus station in the city center, I walked to my hotel along crumbling sidewalks and past shabby, concrete Soviet-era apartment buildings. I went from a luxurious hotel room in Grodno with free Wi-Fi, free laundry service, and made-to-order breakfast to a sparse room in Brest with rough toilet paper, rusty pipes, and one of the saddest excuses for a breakfast buffet I'd ever seen. While receptionists in both Minsk and Grodno greeted me with cheerful smiles and passable English, the women behind the desk in Brest seemed annoyed by my mere presence.

In Brest, I found the tacky commercialism that was blissfully lacking in Minsk and Grodno—ugly signage, chain stores, and kiosks on every corner. Sovetskaya Street, the main pedestrian zone, and Lenin Square were charming, but they were the only parts of the city that appealed to me. One guidebook heartily recommended a stroll by the river, but I turned back after about 15 minutes. Far from scenic, I encountered rows of shabby wooden homes with yards piled high with junk. Aside from one fascinating mural in front of an otherwise nondescript apartment building, Brest felt dismal.

I spent three days in Brest, wondering where I could find all the delightful avenues and charm described in my guidebooks, but aside from Sovetskaya Street and Lenin Square, I came up empty. The only redeeming thing about the city was Brest Fortress. The entrance to the fortress took the shape of a large star. Soviet war anthems, radio broadcasts from World War II, and the sound of gunfire and exploding bombs played ominously as I walked through one point of the star. Brest Fortress was known best for its role in

Operation Barbarossa, during which Soviet troops valiantly defended it against the Germans while they destroyed most of the city. Severely damaged, authorities decided after the war not to rebuild it but to instead create a large memorial to the fight that took place. For history buffs, Brest was where Lenin negotiated the Treaty of Brest-Litovsk with the Germans at the end of World War I.

The centerpiece of Brest Fortress was a 34-meter-tall concrete statue that stood next to an obelisk about 100 meters high. I arrived just in time for the changing of the guard ceremony involving two young women and two young men who stood guard to an eternal flame burning near the base of the obelisk. With white bows billowing at the bottom of the women's braids and the men clearly trying hard not to crack a smile in their unfortunately oversized uniforms, it wasn't exactly the changing of the guard at Buckingham Palace, but I found it amusing nonetheless. Behind the obelisk stood a church with the glimmering gold domes so popular throughout Russia. Elsewhere on the grounds, I found a few other memorials and a collection of tanks, but not much else. After a walk around the outer walls of the fortress, I headed back through the giant concrete star as the booming sounds of bombs exploding bid me farewell.

* * *

After catching a train back to Minsk and meeting up with Yuliya for one last meal, I boarded yet another overnight train. As I once again fell asleep to the *ba-dum-ba-dum-ba-dum* of the train, I reflected on my time in Belarus with mixed emotions. I relished the time I spent with Yuliya and Andrei. I'd grown closer to them than anyone else I'd met on my journey thus far. At the same time, I was heartbroken by so much of what I'd seen, and I was disappointed that Brest didn't live up to its billing. But then I reminded myself that I had arrived in Belarus with almost no expectations and in most ways, it exceeded them. Perhaps I needed to temper my expectations going forward to avoid being let down.

Those thoughts would linger as I headed across the border to Ukraine, where another homestay awaited me.

7
Ukraine

Snow was falling as I stood outside the entrance to a six-story apartment building in the Podil neighborhood of Kyiv. It was 8:30 on a Saturday morning, and I had just arrived on the train from Minsk. Unlike my homestays in St. Petersburg and Moscow, this one was in the heart of the city, just blocks from a metro stop, so it had been an easy trip from the main train station.

I anxiously pressed the intercom buzzer but got no response. Although I informed the language school that arranged this homestay of my early arrival, I'd had no prior contact with my homestay host. I had no idea if she would be expecting me at such an early hour.

Nearly 10 minutes passed before the intercom buzzed back at me, and I heard the click of the door opening. After lugging my bags up four flights of stairs, a tiny blonde woman named Alevtyna, with a squeaky voice and wrinkled skin, welcomed me with a flurry of Russian.

"*Katya? Dobro pozhalovat.* [Katya? Come in]. *Mne ne skazali, chto ty pridesh' tak rano.* [They didn't tell me you were arriving so early]. *Snimay svoyu obuv.* [Take off your shoes]. *Podpisyvaytes' na menya.* [Follow me]."

I took off my shoes and followed Alevtyna inside the small apartment. She led me through the living room to what would be my bedroom for the next two weeks. A large double bed dominated the small space, while a wooden desk was squeezed into a corner. At the foot of the bed, a closet with mirrored sliding doors spanned the width of the room. Oddly, Alevtyna seemed reluctant to show me the kitchen, even though the school assured me I would be able to cook meals for myself since none were included in my homestay fees.

Later that afternoon, Alevtyna sat me down and provided me with a stern lecture in rapid Russian about the dangers of Kyiv. She went on at length about all the criminals and homeless people and repeatedly emphasized how I should not talk to anyone outside of her apartment. Tired and a little shocked, I didn't bother protesting. I just nodded along. Considering how little Russian I'd spoken since leaving Russia, I felt proud that I understood as much of her lecture as I did. It suddenly dawned on me that for the first time since my Trans-Siberian journey, I would be immersed in the Russian language on a full-time basis.

As I settled in, I noticed that Alevtyna had a scale in her bathroom. The morning after I arrived, I nervously weighed myself for the first time in six months. I was dismayed, but not surprised, to see the numbers flash over 74 kilograms—163 pounds, my highest weight ever. I had struggled with my weight and body image since I was a child. As a fourth-grader self-conscious of my chubby cheeks and flabby legs, I wore jeans even on the warmest days so no one could see my thighs jiggle. I slyly tore out articles about calorie counts and exercise from age-inappropriate magazines like *Teen*, *Seventeen*, and *Sassy*. I was only 10 when I started counting calories for the first, but certainly not the last, time.

As an adult, I embarked on one diet after another, never satisfied with the results. But after my relationship with Patrick ended, I threw myself into running and training for my first marathon, losing 15 pounds in the process. I was the thinnest I had been since finishing law school, and my confidence soared. Now, I had gained all that weight back since leaving Chicago, plus a few extra pounds. My pants were even more snug than they had been in Moscow. It was deflating but seeing the number on the scale spurred me into action. I came up with a workout routine to do in my room each morning, consisting of a mix of squats, pushups, kickboxing moves, and strength exercises with a resistance band that I dug out of my backpack for the first time.

Over the next two weeks, I settled into a daily routine, much as I had in Lisiy Nos. After my morning workout and shower, I slogged 20 minutes through the cold and snow to my Russian class each weekday. In a sterile office building in Podil, I spent three hours each morning diving deeper into Russian grammar and expanding my vocabulary. The class was more intimate than my class in St. Petersburg, and the teacher was even friendlier. With no temptation to speak English in my homestay as I had in Russia, I was amazed at how quickly I progressed. I was beginning to even think in Russian.

Nonetheless, I was no match for Alevtyna. She rambled on endlessly, usually speaking too fast for me to understand.

"*Ya ne ponimayu*," I protested repeatedly. "*Govorite pomedlenneye.*"

I implored her to speak more slowly. But the more I told her I didn't understand, the more animated she became. She even grabbed my arm at one point as she tried to yell a Russian word at me loudly enough to make me comprehend. On another occasion, she spent five minutes trying to get me to figure out the Russian word for ice but then stormed out of the galley kitchen without explaining why we were talking about ice in the first place.

Once my Russian class concluded each day, I'd stop at a nearby McDonald's to fill up on French fries, Coke Light, and Wi-Fi. Of course, this was counterproductive to my desire to lose weight, but since Alevtyna didn't have internet, I needed to access Wi-Fi somewhere. I would spend an hour or two replying to emails, publishing new blog posts, and helping a friend manage her website about taking career breaks to travel. I tried to spend my afternoons exploring Kyiv, but the weather didn't cooperate. While the average high in mid-to-late January was in the 20s Fahrenheit, my arrival coincided with the start of 25 straight days of temperatures well below zero. Constant snow also blanketed the city for nine days in a row.

When the snow finally let up, I tried to brave the icy temperatures and see the sights of Kyiv. I had even more free time to wander than I did in St. Petersburg and Moscow, and I was determined not to let the cold stop me. I grew up in Minnesota, after all. I'd already stocked up on long underwear, wool socks, and other winter gear in Russia, so I had the appropriate attire—especially compared to the Ukrainian girls donning short skirts and high-heeled boots and the guys in leather jackets. As I followed a self-guided walking tour through one of Kyiv's parks, the sun was shining bright, and the brisk air felt refreshing. When I stopped to admire the view of the Dnipro River, an elderly man with gold teeth approached me to say hello. He spoke no English, and I struggled to decipher what I assumed was Ukrainian. But his animated facial expressions and gestures told me he wanted to show me around. After following him for about 20 minutes, I can't say I learned much, but it was far more enjoyable than exploring the park solo. I almost forgot about the cold.

The next day, I headed to the Kyivo-Pechers'ka Lavra, not far from the Dnipro River. The cave monastery was actually a collection of golden-domed cathedrals, churches, bell towers and caves. After two hours of walking around the grounds there, I couldn't feel my toes. The calf-high black boots I'd bought in St. Petersburg, while stylish, were not particularly warm or waterproof. By my last Friday in Kyiv, I was struggling to make it more than a few blocks without seeking refuge from the frigid air. I made it to one museum and abandoned my hunt for another because I was chilled to the bone. So much for my Minnesota toughness.

* * *

The cold and snow would not deter me from visiting one of the most unique sites in Ukraine: Chornobyl. I was only nine years old when reactor number four at the Chornobyl power plant outside of Kyiv exploded on April 26, 1986. I probably heard about it on the news when the U.S. government finally learned about it a couple days later. Perhaps it was mentioned in school. I don't remember. Years later, as a college student, I learned about it in the context of contributing to the eventual collapse of the Soviet Union. I would guess that, until recently, the Chornobyl disaster may have been the primary thing many Americans associated with Ukraine.

Shortly after arriving in Kyiv, I learned that it was possible to visit Chornobyl. I met my guide and a group of a dozen other intrepid tourists early one snowy Saturday morning in Kyiv's main square. As we drove about 90 minutes to the exclusion zone, a documentary played on a small screen, providing an overview of the Chornobyl disaster.

The story it told was surprisingly candid, walking through the tragedy minute-by-minute, hour-by-hour. It admitted that Soviet officials tried to cover up the immediate and long-term effects of the blast on the surrounding population. At the same time, it shed light on the issues that officials faced in the days after the explosion—issues that, to my non-scientific ear, sounded eerily like those facing Japan in the days after its 2011 earthquake and subsequent meltdown at the Fukushima power plant.

Our visit began in the 30-kilometer exclusion zone, which included the actual town of Chornobyl. People still lived there, including our tour guide, Vita. However, due to lingering radiation levels, strict controls existed. No children were allowed to live in the zone. The adults who worked in the zone followed "half-on, half-off" schedules. For example,

Vita worked for 15 days, during which time she lived in the zone and then lived in Kyiv for two weeks. In the center of Chornobyl town, a memorial stood in the form of an angel blowing a horn. It referred to a Bible passage that describes the end of days, signaled by seven angels blowing seven horns and a star called Wormwood falling from the sky. Chornobyl is the Ukrainian word for "wormwood." Thus, some believed that the Bible predicted the disaster at the power plant and subsequent contamination.

On our way out of town, we stopped to see some of the military vehicles used in the immediate aftermath of the accident. Although nearly 26 years had passed at the time of my visit, when Vita held a Geiger counter up to the wheel, it still registered higher than normal levels of radiation. I couldn't help but wonder if that was real or just for show.

Our next stop was a kindergarten in a nearby village. I was surprised at the state of the small school, expecting it to look like it did when residents were forced to evacuate, like a place frozen in time. Much to the contrary, it looked like a bomb had exploded in the building, with cracked windows, papers strewn across the floors, and broken chairs and beds scattered throughout the buildings. That said, it clearly wasn't totally abandoned, as one of the newspapers laying around was from 1991.

The same was true when we visited Pripyat, the town closest to the power plant and the first to evacuate after the accident. Sure, there were reminders that no one had lived there since 1986, like a vinyl record in a classroom, a child's report card for the 1985-86 school year, and piles of gas masks on the floor of a school cafeteria—commonplace props in case a nuclear war with the United States began. But I felt more like I was walking through the aftermath of a tornado rather than a building abandoned in a sudden mass evacuation.

Perhaps the biggest reminder that Pripyat was a ghost town was the fact that several feet of snow from the preceding weeks remained completely untouched. Trudging through drifts several feet high, our footprints were the only ones in sight. As we tried to reach the abandoned school, Vita and our driver had to clear snow off the tree branches in front of us.

As we viewed the now-dormant reactors from a distance, I was surprised to find myself sympathizing with government officials who struggled with how to handle the accident. There was no how-to guide in place telling them how to contain the massive fire in reactor number four or how to prevent further explosions from taking place. It also took time for people on the ground to convey information to those making the decisions. There were no mobile phones or wireless internet. Technology was not as advanced as it is now. Things took time. Nonetheless, Soviet officials made the decision to evacuate less than 24 hours after the accident. The following day, they brought in buses and emptied the entire town of 50,000 people in a few hours. I couldn't imagine that happening in the United States. How many people stay behind despite evacuation orders ahead of major hurricanes?

I also thought about the efforts of hundreds of workers who dug a tunnel to install a cooling system underneath the reactor to prevent a further explosion. Such a blast could have been even larger than the first and could have destroyed a large part of Europe. It was terrifying to realize that it could have been so much worse.

* * *

One evening about two weeks into my stay with Alevtyna, I arrived home to find her wandering around the living room in her underwear. She barely gave me a second glance as she retreated to her bedroom, but I took the encounter as a sign that it was time to go. Each of my homestays on the trip had their downsides, but Alevtyna's quirks bothered me the most. She frequently rose in the middle of the night and ran the blender in the kitchen, a noise that pierced my sleep and sometimes continued for 20 to 30 minutes. I came home one day to discover she had taken a plastic bag from my closet and used all my laundry detergent. I also suspected she was using my shampoo. With no patience remaining, I quickly found a hostel in central Kyiv and moved there the next day.

There, I met a cute Australian named Chadwick and developed my first crush of the trip. While I swore I wasn't on an *Eat, Pray, Love*-type journey, it was exhilarating to be attracted to someone again. Chad was my opposite in every way and was likely about 10 years younger than me. While I had painstakingly planned and saved for my trip, he was working at the hostel because he'd run out of money a few months into his gap year. Covered in tattoos and piercings, he was incredibly muscular and frequently wandered around the hostel shirtless, oblivious to the freezing temperatures outside.

Like so many other guys I'd been drawn to in the past, Chad was the life of the party. He also had a way of making everyone he spoke to feel like they were the most important person in the room. Thanks to him, I suddenly had a social life. He invited me to group dinners each evening and insisted I join in as everyone hung out drinking and trading travel stories late into the night. On my last night in Kyiv, Chad organized an outing to one of Kyiv's infamous nightclubs. Clubbing in Kyiv gave me the same knot in my stomach as clubbing in Moscow, but this time I quickly got over my discomfort. Being surrounded by fellow foreigners gave me a sense of belonging that I lacked a few months earlier. None of us wore anything nicer than shabby jeans and sneakers, and we had no connections to get past the bouncers. I didn't care what anyone else thought because we were all in the same boat. For once, I wasn't an outsider.

* * *

It was snowing again as I made my way back to the station in Kyiv to catch a train to L'viv in western Ukraine. I was ready to explore another part of the country—one that would be quite different because, historically, it was never part of the Russian empire. Indeed, western Ukraine was originally part of Poland. During the period between World Wars I and II, most of the region was part of the Second Polish Republic. Other territories belonged to Romania and the Czech Republic. In 1941, much of it became part of the German Third Reich until the end of World War II. At that point, the Soviet Union annexed the region into the Ukrainian Soviet Socialist Republic.

My earliest exposure to Ukrainian politics was in college, working as a research assistant for Professor Vicki Hesli at Iowa. While I'd become obsessed with Russia in high school, Professor Hesli was largely responsible for my fascination with all things Soviet. I took every class she taught, and I was thrilled to assist with her research into the development of democracy and political parties in Ukraine. One thing that stayed with me from that project more than a decade earlier was the stark difference in views between eastern and western Ukraine. The western part of the country was much more amenable to democracy and favored stronger ties with Europe, while the eastern part of the country was decidedly more pro-Russian.

I could feel that difference almost immediately after arriving in L'viv. While everyone I met could understand me and didn't seem to hold it against me that I only spoke Russian, I could tell they all spoke Ukrainian to each other. To my surprise, Polish was often a second or third language on signage in museums and restaurants. The diversity of languages and symbols on the headstones in the Lychakivs'ke Cemetery just outside the city center also spoke to the region's history. Founded in 1787, the cemetery sprawled over several hills in the woods outside of L'viv and included thousands of funerary monuments, angel statues, crosses large and small, and ornate headstones with inscriptions in Polish and Ukrainian. Despite sometimes lumbering through almost knee-high snow, I spent hours exploring this massive cemetery. The white of the snow was broken up only by small bursts of colorful flowers left on gravesites and the orange-red brick of some of the larger monuments.

Before arriving in L'viv, I met Oksana, who ran a travel company called Active Ukraine, through Twitter. She invited me to join her for a class in *pysanky*—traditional Ukrainian egg painting—at the home of one of her guides, Olesia. Egg painting was an ancient tradition, and numerous folk legends and superstitions were associated with the art. Regions, villages, and families all had their own rituals, symbols, and meanings for the painted eggs. I even later visited a museum in the western Ukrainian town of Kolomyya dedicated to *pysanky*, with several thousand eggs on display.

When we arrived at Olesia's apartment, I was surprised to see a carton of eggs sitting on the kitchen table. I thought we would be painting wooden eggs, not real eggs. I was even more surprised to learn that the eggs were not hard-boiled like Easter eggs at home. On the contrary, our first step in the egg painting process was poking a hole in each end of the egg and blowing the yolk and egg white out of the egg. This was not easy. I can't whistle, and I also can't blow anything out of an egg. After about 10 minutes of huffing and puffing with all my might (while being careful not to squeeze the egg too hard and splatter it all over myself), only the slightest bit of egg white dripped out. Sensing that I was a lost cause, Olesia took pity on me and handed me an egg that she had already emptied.

With an empty egg in hand, I was ready to get started. Olesia provided me with a dozen sheets of sample patterns and symbols to inspire the design of my egg. I decided to start by trying to draw just a simple line. But first, I had to master using my stylus. I scooped some wax into a small cup at the top of the stylus and then held it over a candle until the wax melted. Then I used the stylus to etch the melted wax onto the egg.

While Olesia and her two friends made it look incredibly easy, I either used too much wax, and awkward blobs dripped onto my egg, or I didn't have enough wax, so nothing showed up. After what felt like an eternity, I finished my first wobbly line around the egg. Growing in unfounded confidence, I decided to create my own design, featuring a series of flowers. Once I completed the initial design in wax, it was time to dip the egg in yellow dye—the eggs are typically dyed beginning with the lightest color, usually yellow. Everything I etched in wax would remain white.

A few minutes later, I dried off my yellow egg and got to work on the next phase of my design—adding lines inside of my flower petals. Everything I etched at this stage would remain yellow. Although Olesia told me to think happy, positive thoughts while I painted, the perfectionist in me was fighting feelings of frustration. It seemed much harder to paint on the colored egg, and I felt like my attempt at creating an exceptionally fine, detailed design just looked sloppy. It didn't help that my egg started oozing leftover egg white from inside, making things quite messy.

Trying to paint an egg was symbolic of my overall lack of artistic talent—and my sense of perfectionism. Throughout my life, I only pursued something seriously if I was confident that I would be good at it. As a kid, I tried writing poems and then music, but I was pretty much tone-deaf when I tried to sing. I couldn't even master playing a recorder in elementary school, much less a real instrument. My brother had the musical talent in the family, ultimately majoring in musical composition and learning to play multiple instruments, while I never even took piano lessons. I loved art class in junior high, but nothing I did turned out quite as well as I envisioned. As a result, instead of joining the choir or an art club in high school, I threw my energy into two things I excelled at: academics and sports.

The same was true with my egg. While I pictured a beautiful floral pattern in purple, yellow and green, by the time I melted the wax off the egg over a gas burner on Olesia's stove, I was left with a haphazard mess of squiggly lines. When Olesia suggested I paint a second egg, my heart was no longer in it. And I was indifferent when I accidentally crushed my egg while packing to leave L'viv.

* * *

The first thing I noticed as I stared out the dirty marshrutka window winding through the outskirts of Odesa was what was missing: snow. After weeks of snow in Kyiv, freezing temperatures in western Ukraine, and a horrible mix of melting snow, ice, slush, and mud during a week in neighboring Moldova, I felt like spring had arrived as I returned to Ukraine. The sun was shining bright, creating a warmth I hadn't felt in weeks. I strolled through the streets of Odesa with a smile on my face, marveling at architecture that reminded me of St. Petersburg and enjoying the fact that I wasn't slipping on patches of ice or splashing in puddles of slush.

Odesa was a major port on the Black Sea, founded by Catherine the Great at the end of the 18th century and eventually home to one of the largest Jewish populations in the Russian empire. I saw most of the major city highlights on the afternoon I arrived: the gorgeous baroque Opera House and the founders statue in Ekaterininskaya Square; the quaint pedestrian Deribasivs'ka Street and the artsy Soborna Square; the Mother-in-Law Bridge covered with padlocks placed by lovestruck couples; and the giant staircase known as the Potemkin Stairs that served as the entrance to the city from the sea. Perhaps it was just the contrast to the dreary cold I experienced for a week in Moldova, but Odesa felt magical. I wished I had planned for more than just a couple days there.

On my second morning in Odesa, one email changed my whole mood. As soon as I saw the subject line, I knew it was bad news. I paused a minute or two before opening, but that wasn't enough to prepare me for what I was about to read: "I am so sorry to have to break this news by email when you're away, but we had to put Leo down today."

Leo was my darling orange tabby cat who I adopted eight years earlier. He was the second of two cats I adopted from shelters after my mom put my childhood cat to sleep while I was away on a summer internship during law school. The first had been Wally. A blue-eyed Siamese, Wally knew he was beautiful and expected everyone to shower him with affection. After dragging him from Minnesota to Chicago with me after law school, I started to feel guilty over how much time he spent alone while I was at my big firm lawyer job. I stopped at an adoption event at a local pet store and found Leo, named after Leonardo DaVinci since I was reading *The Da Vinci Code* at the time. My first childhood cat was an orange tabby and so was Leo. It was love at first sight. To my great relief, Wally and Leo soon became best buddies, and I could spend hours watching them wrestle, fight, cuddle, and clean each other. It was hard to imagine I would ever be without them.

Then I started planning my career break trip. Although I'd first started thinking of quitting my job to travel nearly two years earlier, I formally announced it to the world by email exactly six months before I left. That email set off a flurry of activity, from selling my belongings to finding a tenant for my condominium to picking up odd jobs online to make extra money and hit my savings goal. For a long time, I didn't want to think about the fact that I would need to give up my cats; it was too hard.

A couple months after announcing my departure plans, I realized Wally was not his normal self. I was changing the litter box much more frequently. I was refilling the water bowl multiple times a day when it used to never run dry. Wally felt a lot lighter when I picked him up, and I could feel the bones of his spine jutting out when I petted him. Finally, to knock myself out of denial, I stepped on the scale with him and realized he had lost about five pounds, which is a lot for a cat. Something was wrong. A trip to the vet confirmed my worst fear: Wally had diabetes.

Even if I wasn't leaving, that would've been a hard diagnosis to take. My plans made it even harder. I could try to take care of Wally for a few months, but it was going to be enough of a challenge to find a new home for two older but healthy cats. Who was going to take in a 13-year-old cat with diabetes? I knew deep down that the logical thing was to put Wally to sleep, but I felt like I was a horrible, selfish person to even consider it. My dad reassured me that, while

I had done some selfish things in my life, this would not be one of them.

I talked to the vet and explained the circumstances. He very kindly, but unsuccessfully, tried to find someone to foster Wally. And then he called me on a Friday evening and concurred that it was best to go ahead and put Wally to sleep. I spent one last weekend with him and then took him in on a Monday afternoon. As I set out the cat carrier, he didn't fight me; he seemed to know it was time. The tears started rolling before I even got to the vet's office, but the staff was wonderful, and it was almost a relief when it was finally over. The vet assured me again that I had done the right thing.

And then I went home to Leo, who didn't understand why his buddy for the last eight years wasn't coming back. Seeing his confusion and loneliness was almost as hard as saying goodbye to Wally. I hoped that the silver lining in putting Wally to sleep would be that it would be easier to find someone to take just Leo when it was time for me to leave. Luckily, I was right. My friend Patty and her husband had been thinking of getting a cat to be a companion for their dog Jack once their new baby came. A few weeks later, I took Leo to their place to test the waters. We were surprised and relieved when there was no hissing, growling, or snarling—just some tentative stares and curious sniffing. A couple weeks after that, I packed up the litter box and the cat food and pushed an unhappy Leo into his cat carrier to make the trip to his new home.

It seemed like an ideal situation. Leo was starved for companionship since Wally left, so I was hopeful that he and Jack would get along well over time. And I was relieved that I was able to find a friend to take Leo instead of resorting to a random person on Craigslist or, even worse, leaving him at an animal shelter. It was a tough transition at first. Leo spent the first month hiding in a far corner under a bed, only lured out by the promise of tuna. But eventually, he came out and seemed to blend in well with his new family. Patty sent me pictures of Leo and Jack lying on the bed together and told me how he let their new baby tug at him as she crawled around. I was thrilled and relieved that it seemed to be working out so well. Around Thanksgiving, with my return date unknown, Patty and I agreed they would permanently adopt Leo.

But now, not even three months later, as I lay in a hostel bed in Odesa, I was reading about how Leo had stopped eating and had been losing weight and how the vet initially thought it might be kidney disease but then concluded diabetes. It all sounded so familiar, and reading it broke my heart all over again. I'd hated making the decision to put Wally to sleep, even though everyone assured me it was the right call. After reading about the same thing happening with Leo, I couldn't help but wonder if the stress of everything triggered his illness. When I'd taken him to the vet in June, he was given a clean bill of health. It was so hard to understand how he became so sick so fast. And as with Wally, I couldn't help but feel guilty and selfish—that if I hadn't given him up to go on my trip, he'd still be alive and purring. And I felt bad that my friends had to deal with the decision of putting him down—it certainly wasn't what they signed up for.

The tears started flowing before I even finished reading the email, and they didn't stop for almost four hours. I surprised myself with how long I cried, but it felt like a healthy, necessary cry. I wasn't just mourning Leo. In a way, I was mourning everything else I gave up pursuing this trip—my job, my friends, my former life. As I lay alone on my tiny hostel bed, thankful that I had booked a private room, I wondered if it was all worth it.

8
The Black Sea & Georgia

"Miss Kaaaahteeee!"

A thin, balding Ukrainian man flashed me a large smile as he extended his hand to shake mine. I was standing in the middle of the doorway to a small, unremarkable office in an old apartment building in the center of Odesa.

This must be Vladlen, I thought as I grasped his hand for a firmer-than-normal handshake. I had been exchanging emails with Vladlen for a couple months, trying to sort out the logistics of taking a ferry from Odesa across the Black Sea to the country of Georgia. Finally, I could put a face with the name.

"Sit, sit," he urged me.

I sat down across from Vladlen, a pale green metal desk separating us. I handed him my passport together with 1,450 Ukrainian hryvna (about $180). He explained in broken English how I should make my way from Odesa to the ferry office in a village called Burlachya Balka. He emphasized that I should be there promptly at 2 p.m. It was already 11 a.m. when I left his office, so I stopped quickly at the grocery store to buy some snacks, visited a bank to exchange most of my remaining hryvna, and ate at Puzata Hata, my favorite cafeteria-style Ukrainian restaurant one last time for lunch.

By noon, I checked out of my hostel and headed to the busy train station to catch a bus toward Ilyichevsk. Although Vladlen told me it would take one hour, the driver motioned to me after just 30 minutes that we were at my stop. I walked into the lobby of a brand-new office building seemingly in the middle of nowhere and saw only a stone-faced woman sitting behind a cashier's window. After checking my passport, she handed me a boarding pass and told me to wait. An hour later, a minibus arrived to take me to the customs and immigration office, along with an older Ukrainian gentleman and a young German hitchhiker named Paul. After a short drive, we were ushered into a poorly lit room with about 20 other people waiting for the border control to check our passports. Officers questioned us twice, both times in English.

"How long you have been in Ukraine?" the first officer inquired. I paused, overthinking whether to include only the last few days or the several weeks I spent in the country before my side trip to Moldova. I had barely stammered "three" when he was on the next question.

"How much hryvna? Dollars?"

"Do you have any medicines?"

As the first officer waved me ahead, a second officer asked me again, "How long you have been in Ukraine?"

I nodded and he continued, "You come from Moldova?"

"*Da*," I replied in Russian, now a habit for me.

"How long in Moldova?"

"Why do you go to Georgia?"

"Where do you go after Georgia?"

An hour later, we all climbed onto a bus that took us to the actual Black Sea ferry—a sizable vessel that was a combination cargo ship and passenger ferry. I managed to snap a few pictures before a baby-faced teenager decked out in a military uniform nicely scolded me, "No photo."

Once aboard the boat, I reluctantly turned over my passport at reception for the duration of the journey. A steward led me through a maze of hallways to my room—a spacious four-person cabin where, to my surprise, Paul was sitting on a small sofa next to the porthole. I'd never considered that I might have a roommate. After my long train rides in cramped compartments, this room was a luxury with comfortable twin-size beds, a large table, and an en-suite bathroom. As a bonus, it was on the eighth level, so it included a nice view out of the front of the boat.

Dinner that evening was served in the seventh-floor restaurant. Although Vladlen had told me it would be cafeteria-style, Paul and I arrived to find all the plates already set with rice and chicken, a pickle, and salad. Like a normal cruise ship, we had assigned seating, which seemed to be based on nationality. Paul sat at table number five with a group of German truck drivers. As the only American on board, I sat at table number 11 with a group of Georgians. As I scanned the room during dinner, I noticed that I was one of just seven women on the boat, out of about 70 passengers. I was also one of the youngest. Serving primarily as a vehicle ferry, most passengers were truck drivers accompanying their large semi-trucks across the sea. When I went up on deck the next day to take some pictures, I realized many of the trucks carried livestock as drivers were going in to feed their "cargo."

Despite boarding mid-afternoon, it was close to midnight when we finally set sail. Paul and I stood with the window open, a cold sea breeze blowing in, and watched as we slowly passed by all the lights in the harbor and drifted out into the open sea. As I fell asleep that first night, I was amazed at how smooth and quiet the ride was. We left the curtain open at night, so we awoke the next morning with the sunrise. Breakfast was served promptly at 8 a.m., after which I returned to the cabin to read before falling asleep for a couple hours. I hadn't realized until then how much the previous few weeks had worn me out. I was also pleasantly surprised to discover the 3G on my Kindle worked as we passed by Crimea midday—the last land we would see for two days.

I didn't spend much time outside of the cabin over the next couple days. I felt like I needed the rest and I saw the journey as the perfect time to catch up on reading, writing, and editing photos without any distractions. The truck drivers on board were also an intimidating bunch. Most spoke French, German, or Georgian rather than English or even Russian, so a complete language barrier divided us. Most of the common areas allowed smoking and just walking through the TV lounge to the restaurant irritated my eyes and made me cough. I could also feel the eyes of a dozen men on me every time I passed by. My entire body stiffened, an inherent reaction to my perception that they were ridiculing or laughing at me.

By the second day, everything started to feel routine, like afternoon naps and concise announcements in Russian inviting us to the restaurant for each meal. Paul and I thought we might arrive in Batumi as early as that evening, but since land was not even in sight as the sun went down, we assumed it would be Sunday morning instead. We got our first clue that we may be delayed beyond Sunday morning when we went down for breakfast and saw a menu posted for the entire day.

Sure enough, shortly before lunch, they announced that the Port of Batumi was closed. My heart sank a bit at that point. It was Sunday afternoon, my third day on the ferry, and I was getting antsy. I had finished all the writing I wanted to do, read two books, and exhausted all topics of conversation with Paul. We covered the "where are you from, what do you do, where are you going" niceties on the first night and didn't seem to have much more in common beyond our status as the only tourists on the ferry.

While we'd traversed similar routes through Europe, Paul was hitchhiking with no set schedule or destination. As I shared what I loved most in Riga or Vilnius or Kyiv, he just gave me a blank look; sightseeing wasn't a priority for him. He also didn't understand why I was so stressed about potentially being stuck on the ferry for extra days. I tried to explain that I was supposed to go to the Azerbaijan embassy first thing Monday morning to apply for my Azeri visa, which would take three business days to process. Needing to be in Yerevan, Armenia by the weekend to start a long-planned volunteer experience meant I was under a time crunch. He replied with a callous, "So what?"

I soon learned from the English-speaking bartender that the port was closed due to high winds and that we may arrive as early as Sunday night or perhaps not until Monday morning. But Monday morning brought more bad weather, with hail, wind, and rain blowing in just after breakfast. As a chubby Georgian named Kvicha was hitting on me and insisting I take his phone number, they announced that the port was still closed. I wanted to cry. While the romantic overtures of my new friend were amusing, if not a little creepy, I was getting close to my breaking point. However, by early Monday evening, the skies had cleared, and I watched with excitement as we headed straight for the shore. The lights of the city of Batumi glittered in the distance and I was already thinking about what I would do once I had settled into my guesthouse.

We docked just after 7 p.m. and they called everyone down to reception to return their room keys and pick up their passports. Paul and I tore the linens off our beds, packed up our things and hauled our backpacks down to the smoky reception area to wait for the next step. And then we waited.

After what felt like an eternity, they announced that we weren't getting off the boat after all. There was some sort of problem with the ramp, which meant we had to stay on board until morning. I heard this news from Paul, who heard it from one of the German truck drivers. I thought he was kidding, just trying to get a rise out of me. I swore at him, and when I realized it was all real, I broke down crying. I didn't understand why the non-driver passengers couldn't leave if it was just the vehicle ramp that was broken. Even the drivers initially thought that Paul and I would get to leave.

Just when I thought it couldn't get any worse, Paul drank himself into a stupor. After a night of vodka shots with the German truck drivers, he stumbled into the cabin around 2 a.m., knocking things over, repeatedly mumbling, "God is great," in German, and eventually writing the same phrase in black marker on the wall above his bed. When I asked what he was doing, he stopped and bolted out of the room. I lay in bed, terrified of his eventual return. He seemed to be in a crazed state, and it would not have surprised me if he'd plunged overboard. He returned an hour later, falling over every step. His mumbling turned into chanting, and he punched the wall several times, knocking the headboard down, before curling up on his bed in the fetal position and bursting into tears.

I tried to stay completely still, not wanting Paul to realize I was awake. Eventually, he passed out, but not without some more chants in his sleep. When the sun rose the next morning, he jumped into the shower, clearly still drunk, mumbling, and making all sorts of weird noises. Then he grabbed the blanket off his bed and disappeared again. As soon as he was gone, I got up and looked out the window to see dark skies, rain blowing sideways, and waves crashing against the side of the boat. I completely lost it.

I was so tired of being on the boat. Tired of Paul, even before his drunken escapade. Tired of not having anyone else to speak with in English. Tired of not being able to eat half the food because it contained gluten. Tired of my stomach rumbling because I'd run out of snacks after two days and they didn't sell any on board. Tired of being cut off from the rest of the world aside from very brief stints of 3G access on my Kindle. Tired of stressing over getting my Azeri visa and tired of working through different scenarios in my head of how I would get myself to Tbilisi and then on to Yerevan to start my volunteer assignment on time. Tired of truck drivers staring at me as I walked through the smoky reception area. Tired of our bathroom that smelled worse than the outhouse I had to use during my homestay in St. Petersburg. At that moment, I had never wanted anything so badly as to get off that boat.

After crying my eyes out all Tuesday morning, I turned a corner by late that afternoon. I hate to give Paul any credit, but in his hungover state, he gave me a lecture I probably needed to hear.

"Delays happen," he reminded me. "This is part of traveling. It is part of the adventure. Just go with the flow."

"Why not make the most of this time?" Paul continued. "Don't waste your energy being upset. Think about the good times on your journey so far. Don't focus on the bad."

While it was my nature to focus on the bad—the disappointing homestays, frequent loneliness, and freezing my butt off for three weeks in Ukraine—I had to admit that Paul made some good points. And did I focus on the negative because I expected too much in the first place? Were my expectations unreasonable? Perhaps they were. I resolved to make the most of whatever time I had left on the boat. By Tuesday evening, I had finalized a few blog posts, edited all my photos, and started reading a third book. At dinner that night, I was thrilled when they served ice cream for dessert—my first sweets in four days! I went to bed confident that we would finally reach port and disembark Wednesday morning.

Sure enough, I awoke the next day to cloudless blue skies, and by 8 a.m., we were approaching Batumi. I went up on deck to take pictures and enjoy the view of the city in the daytime. As I did, one of the Georgian truck drivers, Tomas, approached me. We chatted in Russian and I learned that he thought Paul and I were married. When I told him that we weren't and that I was single, he hugged me and kissed me on the cheek. Soon, I had Tomas' phone number to go along with Kvicha's that I got on Monday. Then I met Ilya and had almost an identical conversation with the same reaction. A few minutes later, I encountered Tomas, Kvicha, and another Georgian in the hallway near the cabins, and they all insisted on taking pictures with me. Finally, I met an older Georgian woman named Londa, who invited me to stay with her in Tbilisi and gave me her phone numbers in both Georgia and Ukraine.

Before I knew it, the boat had docked, and I returned to the reception area to go through immigration formalities. As I stepped up to the counter and handed over my American passport, the officer greeted me with a smile.

"Ahhhh, America! Welcome! You are always welcome here!"

"*Spasibo*," I replied with an equally large grin.

"Noooo. *Madloba. Mad-loh-ba*," he corrected me, sharing the Georgian word for "thank you."

The officer then taught me how to say hello—*gamarjoba*—as well. We shared several laughs as I repeated both after him several times. It was possibly the warmest welcome I have ever received in a country and gave me a feeling of optimism as I started my travels through the Caucasus: Georgia, Armenia and Azerbaijan.

When I finally set foot on dry land and waved goodbye to Kvicha, Tomas, and Londa, I couldn't help but think how much more I would have enjoyed the entire journey if I had met them the first day instead of the last. What kind of connections could I have formed if I hadn't let myself be intimidated by the other passengers? What if I had stopped worrying about what they thought of me and pushed my negative perceptions out of my head?

This was not a new feeling for me. There were certainly times when I welcomed new, potentially uncomfortable experiences, like when I went on the ski trip to Austria with 30 strangers that led to meeting Patrick or when I took an improv class and performed in front of 700 people. But too often, I froze with insecurity and failed to make the most of opportunities right in front of me. Taking a cargo ferry across the Black Sea was certainly pushing the limits of my comfort zone, but I realized that once I got on board, I crawled into a shell rather than fully embracing the adventure in front of me. Indeed, this entire journey should have been about expanding my boundaries, but I wondered whether I was making the most of it. The question for me as I arrived in Batumi was whether I would apply anything I'd learned on the ferry going forward.

*　*　*

I sat on the bottom bunk of yet another overnight train,

this time going from Batumi to Tbilisi, the capital of Georgia. As usual, I boarded early and found myself sitting and waiting to see who might join me in my four-person *kupe*. I was still mentally exhausted from my Black Sea ferry experience and was hoping for a quiet ride. A gray-haired Georgian man was the first to join me, settling quietly into the other bottom bunk without acknowledging my presence. A few minutes later, a young, skinny Georgian guy in a black leather jacket strutted in, setting a plastic bag on the small table next to me before walking out. I cringed when I saw a bottle of liquor peeking out the top of the bag. As a woman traveling solo, I didn't love the idea of sharing a cramped compartment with one or more drunk Georgian men.

"Do you speak Georgian?"

I looked up to see the older man on the other bottom bunk looking at me, awaiting a response.

"No," I replied. "But I speak some Russian."

"*Khorosho!*" the man exclaimed with a warm smile. "*Kak vas zovut? Menya zovut Merabe.*"

"*Menya zovut Katya,*" I introduced myself, suddenly feeling more at ease. Months into my trip, I was feeling more like Katya—the Russified version of my real name—than Katie.

It turned out that Merabe was Georgian but lived in Mallorca, Spain. He spoke Georgian, Russian, English, and Spanish. He peppered me with questions until the young guy returned, this time with a friend by his side. Merabe explained to them in Georgian who I was and where I was from. Neither spoke much Russian, but neither spoke any English either, so Merabe served as an interpreter. As soon as the train left the station, the skinny guy, Misha, pulled out his bottle of Georgian cognac and handed us each a small plastic cup. His friend David followed with pineapple juice, paprika-flavored Lay's potato chips, and a chocolate bar—our chasers. My initial trepidation turned into measured anticipation. I was finally going to experience the craziness of an overnight train that the Trans-Siberian failed to deliver.

Merabe explained that the day was March 8—International Women's Day. I had never heard of it, but I thought the concept was a great one—recognizing and appreciating women. However, I soon got the impression that the men just saw it as an excuse to drink. Indeed, at the first stop, Merabe disappeared and returned with a second bottle of cognac, signaling it would be a long night on the train to Tbilisi! As soon as Misha poured the first shots, the guys started a series of toasts in Georgian, and Merabe translated for me in a mix of Russian, English, and Spanish. They toasted to me, to their mothers and sisters, and to all the women in the world—multiple times. Every toast was incredibly long, and by the fourth shot, it was my turn to toast. I did my best in Russian, saying it was wonderful meeting them and toasting to Georgia. After more toasts and more shots, David pulled out his cell phone and started playing what he explained was a traditional song from the region of Adjara, where Batumi was located and where David and Misha lived.

Suddenly, Misha jumped up and started dancing in the middle of our compartment. A few minutes later, David took his turn, and eventually, I got pulled into the fray as well, doing my best attempt at Georgian dancing. After a few shots, I knew I was reaching my limit and started declining when Misha went to refill my cup. Instead, he just poured slightly less, saying, "*choot-choot.*" I took small sips as a chorus of toasts continued. Eventually, we ran out of cognac and things started to quiet down. As we talked more, Merabe suggested I stay with his mother-in-law's family in Telavi and his wife in Batumi when I returned to Georgia. He even called both to give them a heads-up. Then he offered his brother to drive me to Armenia on Sunday and insisted he introduce us the next day. I didn't feel comfortable taking him up on his offers, but I appreciated the hospitality nonetheless.

By 2 a.m., Misha climbed up into his top bunk without saying a word, signaling it was time to call it a night. Our train pulled into Tbilisi just a few hours later. As we exited the train, Misha grabbed my large backpack, struggling to hoist it onto his skinny back. I joined him and David for much-needed tea at the station before they insisted on accompanying me to the subway. I had just one stop to go before I grabbed my backpack from Misha and hopped off the train, waving them a fond farewell. It was the perfect, unexpected welcome to Georgia, and it showed me what could happen if I opened myself up more to people along the way.

As much as I enjoyed meeting Olga, Maarten and Mariann, and Yuliya and Andrei, I found myself holding back. I was wary of imposing on anyone. This was especially true with men I met along the way. I often let my insecurities take over as I tried to balance a perceived need to keep my guard up as a woman traveling solo with my desire to connect with new people. My time on the ferry and the train gave me a confidence boost, and meeting men like Merabe, David and Misha showed me perhaps I could find the right balance between being open and cautious.

9
Armenia

Still wiping the sleep from my eyes, I crammed into a minivan with a dozen other volunteers and settled in for the long ride south out of Yerevan. It was a Saturday morning about halfway into my six-week stay in Armenia. We were on our way to Tatev Monastery and the village of Tandzatap for the weekend. I was excited to explore more of Armenia's natural beauty and ancient history. I was also looking forward to the chance to bond with my fellow volunteers, something that really hadn't happened yet.

I'd arrived in Yerevan, the capital of Armenia, three weeks earlier after a short stay in Tbilisi. I was full of excitement to start a volunteer placement with the Armenian Volunteer Corps. AVC appealed to me because it was a local organization that placed volunteers based on their professional backgrounds, skills, and interests. I was assigned to the National Competitiveness Foundation of Armenia, in its tourism division. As a travel blogger harboring vague dreams of starting some kind of travel business, it seemed perfect. After my run of dissatisfying volunteer opportunities, I was eager to turn the tide.

While AVC accepted volunteers of all ages and ethnicities, its sister organization, Birthright Armenia, focused on the diaspora—ethnic Armenians ages 20 to 32 who grew up outside the country. The two organizations shared offices and the staff seemed interchangeable. Birthright offered excursions and language classes in which AVC volunteers were welcome to participate, which was how I found myself in a minivan on the way to southern Armenia on a Saturday morning. I hadn't given the existence of AVC and Birthright as two separate organizations much thought prior to arriving, so I hadn't considered the possibility that I might be the only non-ethnic Armenian volunteer—or that it would matter.

I quickly realized that the other volunteers connected with each other in ways that I just could not. Some had already been in Armenia for months and forged strong friendships; others seemed to click immediately upon arrival. They shared a common culture, heritage, and language. While visiting Armenia was an interesting stop for me on my year-long career break, it meant so much more to them. I would compare it to me visiting Norway or Germany (home to my paternal ancestors), but Armenia, for them, was clearly more powerful. My ancestors didn't flee due to war or genocide. I didn't grow up hearing stories from my parents about the homeland or speaking Norwegian or attending German school. They were experiencing things in Armenia in a way I could never fully understand.

I also didn't expect that I would be the only one over 30. I felt like I was in a much different place in my life than the other volunteers, and I struggled to find common ground. Most of the others had recently finished college or graduate school and were taking time to volunteer and explore their roots before moving on with their careers. They were doing what I wished I'd done 10 years earlier. I envied them that they took advantage of an opportunity that I couldn't pursue at that age. It's not that people weren't friendly; like the concept of "Minnesota Nice" where I grew up, everyone was welcoming on the surface, but at the same time, I didn't feel like they fully included me. When it came to breaking into a close-knit group full of inside jokes and shared experiences, my insecurities took over and I shut down. Just as I so often did as a teenager, I felt like I was on the outside looking in.

Beyond that, for the first time, I was experiencing true "language shock." Arriving in Armenia made me realize how comfortable I'd become speaking and reading Russian. Suddenly, I was in a situation where not only did I not understand the language, but I also couldn't read the alphabet. While I was taking Armenian lessons twice a week, my teacher didn't even try to teach me to read because she thought it was too difficult; the Armenian alphabet was like no other in the world.

Not knowing Armenian made me feel helpless. I couldn't read the signs on the marshrutkas to see where they went, making it harder to get around. I couldn't read the menus in most fast-food restaurants, leaving me to eat half my meals at KFC because I at least knew how to order chicken kebabs, fries, and coleslaw. Indeed, the cashier at KFC soon memorized my order. People told me that everyone understood Russian in Yerevan, but my initial attempts to speak

Russian were either ignored or met with scowls. When I tried to use the few words I knew in Armenian, no one seemed to understand because my pronunciation was off.

Everyone I met in Yerevan also seemed suspicious of my intentions in coming to Armenia. No one understood why a blonde American with no Armenian roots would want to visit their country. This doubt was new to me. No one in Estonia questioned why I would visit Estonia, and no Lithuanians seemed to find it odd that I would spend two weeks in Vilnius. While many Russians thought my desire to ride the Trans-Siberian Railway was bizarre, no one thought twice about my reasons for visiting St. Petersburg or Moscow. But for some reason, in Armenia, people seemed to think I was incredibly weird for wanting to visit. Even the guy who sold me my visa at the border raised his eyebrows at the fact that I requested a visa for longer than the standard 21 days.

The one bright spot was meeting a fellow volunteer named Andy. From the moment we were introduced at an Irish pub on St. Patrick's Day, he drew me in with his engaging smile and dark, welcoming eyes. He was soft-spoken yet always the center of attention—the kind of guy that put everyone at ease. Our conversations quickly moved from superficial niceties to deeper topics like religion and politics. I knew he was quite a bit younger than me—everyone was—but I had no idea how much. I didn't want it to matter. While I had a crush on Chad in Kyiv, the feeling there was not mutual. With Andy, I felt like I had found a connection with a guy that had been missing for so long, both at home and on the road. I was determined to make the most of it.

* * *

When we arrived in Tandzatap, a village of about 70 families, we split into small groups and settled into a half dozen homestays. I'd been paired with Annie, another volunteer, and Anton, one of the Birthright staff members. We started our evening by learning how to prepare *khoravats*—Armenian barbecue. Once the *khoravats* was on the grill, we went to visit each of the homestays. This gave us a chance to see the entire village and gave me a chance to make some new friends. Eventually, everyone came together in the village hall for an enormous meal accompanied by plenty of vodka shots. Over the next few hours, we drank and danced and watched the old village men dance with far more skill than we had. Many volunteers honed their Armenian skills by chatting with the villagers while I practiced my Russian as best I could with the elders. I also took every opportunity to be near Andy without being too obvious about it. I beamed as Andy's homestay host seemed to try to play matchmaker between us, inviting me to come to their house for a nightcap. Knowing I'd already hit my vodka limit and, wary of sparking any gossip, I reluctantly declined.

I awoke to the sound of roosters crowing the next morning. After a breakfast of eggs and tea, Annie and I went for a walk to photograph Tandzatap in the warm, glowing sun. Chickens and cows greeted us as we wandered. From the end of the village, we could see all the way to Tatev Monastery at the top of the Vorotan Gorge. Soon, most of our group gathered to hike into the gorge. We set off along a slippery path covered with a mix of ice, snow, mud, and cow manure. Keeping our balance was tricky, and it wasn't long before the trail claimed its first victim. Andy lost his footing just minutes after we joked about not taking each other down if we fell. The messy conditions didn't last long, but we were soon met with another foe—thorny branches blocking the path. By the time we reached the bottom of the gorge, I'd stopped multiple times to pick splinters out of my ankles, and I was covered with scratches.

From the bottom of the gorge, we climbed up a short distance to reach the 17th century Mets Anapat monastery. With free time to explore, everyone went their separate ways. Annie and Angela found a spot on the grass-covered monastery roof to nap. Serena snapped pictures in every direction while Kurt practiced yoga. I made a loop around the monastery before settling on the grassy roof to enjoy an apple and bask in the spring sunshine. After a while, I spotted Andy down below, and he raised his camera to take my picture.

"Beautiful," he said with a smile.

I grinned from ear to ear as I felt my face turn red. I hoped he was too far away to notice.

It felt special to have the monastery to ourselves, and it was hard to leave when it was finally time to move on. I don't think any of us were prepared for how difficult the hike back out of the gorge would be—steep paths that often weren't really paths, thorny branches blocking our way and loose rocks that crumbled below our feet. We concluded our adventure by carefully crossing the unstable remains of a rockslide and then sliding down a hill of pure dirt and rocks to the main road, where our vans awaited.

Still just early afternoon, we moved on to Goris, a

picturesque city set in a valley surrounded by mountains full of medieval cave dwellings. After lunch at a hilltop restaurant overlooking the city, we explored the surrounding rock formations and caves. I wandered off on my own, hoping Andy might follow, but he was nowhere to be found. I was happy, then, when we finally packed into the vans for the five-hour ride back to Yerevan. Wiped out from the drinking, dancing, and hiking over the past 24 hours, it was a mellow journey. I manipulated my way into sitting next to Andy. We chatted quietly for nearly two hours before I dozed off with my head on his shoulder.

* * *

I sat in Patricia's apartment, sipping red wine and trying not to look at Andy. It was the Friday before Easter and most of the AVC and Birthright volunteers were gathered to celebrate the long weekend by drinking wine, coloring eggs, and playing a variety of games that brought me back to my college days, including a version of "I Never." Perhaps it was my imagination, but I constantly felt Andy's eyes on me, and he always seemed to end up near me. When we eventually left Patricia's to go to Calumet, our go-to bar in Yerevan, we walked most of the way together. Once there, the vodka went down quickly and the dancing was in full swing. One minute, people were grinding to the latest Katy Perry hit and the next, they were dancing arm-in-arm to a traditional Armenian favorite. I tried to play it cool as Andy danced awkwardly behind me. I didn't think my crush was obvious at this point, and I really didn't want it to be. At the same time, my heart sank a little every time he danced near anyone else.

Soon, Andy took a break, sitting on a nearby bench. I summoned the nerve to sit down next to him. As was typical for me, once I found myself attracted to a guy, I lost almost all ability to initiate conversation. In this case, though, I didn't need to. Andy stood up and grabbed my hand, pulling me back to the dance floor. By this time, it was well past midnight and the bar had mostly emptied out. When Andy pulled me close to him to dance, I went along with it, but as he leaned in close to kiss me, I pulled back. It was one thing to dance with him in the middle of the bar; it was quite another to kiss him.

After several songs, we stopped dancing as Andy's friend David came over to talk to us. The bar was closing, so we followed David outside and watched as he jumped into a taxi. We stood hip-to-hip on the sidewalk, Andy with his hands on my lower back, staring into my eyes and smiling. And finally, I let him kiss me.

The kiss seemed to last for hours and was everything I had been hoping for—until Andy's roommate Jeff appeared out of nowhere and awkwardly tapped him on the shoulder. Jeff offered to stay elsewhere, so Andy and I could go back to their place. At that moment, there was nothing I wanted more. But in the back of my drunken mind, I knew I shouldn't. I was in Armenia, living with host parents who would likely freak out if I wasn't there in the morning. I didn't want to make them worry. I also didn't want to be the subject of gossip among the close-knit group of volunteers that I was just starting to connect with. My 35-year-old self was just as self-conscious as I'd been in my teens and 20s and just as insecure when it came to the opposite sex. So instead, I opened the door to a taxi that had just pulled up next to us and whispered to Andy, "Another time."

The next morning, I awoke to the blinding sun shining in my bedroom. As I sat up, a wave of giddiness came over me. Did last night really happen? Did Andy really kiss me? I couldn't remember the last time I felt so attracted to a guy so quickly. Indeed, I'd begun to wonder if I was even capable of feeling that butterflies-in-your-stomach level of excitement about someone again. And while I continued to tell myself this trip was about finding myself, not finding love, would it really be so bad if I enjoyed a romance along the way?

* * *

I smiled as my Blackberry buzzed the next evening. I had spent the day exploring Yerevan, finally visiting the Yerevan History Museum and wandering through the market, shopping for souvenirs as my time in Armenia was winding down. I didn't think I'd hear from Andy, so I was thrilled to see an invitation from him to join a group out at a jazz club. Not wanting to arrive alone, I recruited another volunteer, Lillian, to join me. By the time we arrived, Andy was settled into a corner booth, Angela on one side and Jeff on the other. Lillian and I ended up far across the table.

Suddenly, a feeling of discomfort came over me. I wondered who knew about the previous night. I pondered how much Andy even remembered. I grew even more anxious as Lillian turned our conversation toward guys and dating, and she asked if I had kissed anyone since I'd been in

Armenia. Did she know about Andy and me, and was she trying to get me to admit it? I laughed and shook my head no.

Eventually, Andy caught my eye and raised his glass to me, breaking the ice. When we left to go to the next bar, he waited for me, and we walked together, settling again into easy conversation. I felt a huge sense of relief. The attraction I had felt for weeks was not all in my head. The scene repeated itself the following night, and we found ourselves back at Calumet.

Once there, we picked up dancing again, this time to Adele's "Someone Like You."

As Andy held me close, I whispered, "I was afraid things might be weird between us after Friday."

"Why would it be weird?" he responded, raising his thick eyebrows in surprise.

"I don't know," I replied, even though I could have listed half a dozen reasons. "I'm glad it's not."

The truth was, I was terrified that things had become weird, and I was flailing with self-doubt. It was the story of my life. I'd meet a great guy and then misread signals and ignore signs as I convinced myself the feeling was mutual, only to discover it wasn't. This pattern was far too familiar as I managed to have my heart broken in an increasingly disappointing fashion. High school, college, law school, and beyond. Jeremy. Eric. Brandon. Brad. Curt. Matt. Joe. Rob. Zach. Patrick. One guy after the next, the outcome was always the same. Of course, it was my heartbreak from Patrick that had indirectly led to me being in Armenia in the first place.

Patrick was far from my mind as Andy pulled me close on the dance floor, but the insecurities created by my breakup with him, and so many before him, weighed heavily. Was it too much to ask to have a guy chase me for a change?

* * *

Andy was slightly slurring his words when Lillian and I arrived at the small apartment he shared with Jeff on my last Friday in town. I'd seen him nearly every day my last week in Yerevan, but always in a group setting: happy hours, pub trivia, and a flag football game. As much as I feared that people were secretly judging me for kissing Andy, I simultaneously felt more included than ever as Jeff seemed to make a point to invite me to everything. To my surprise, no one questioned my sudden presence. And while Andy and I spent plenty of time together during these group activities—enough for me to stop questioning if he liked me back—I was craving some alone time with him before I left for Georgia to continue my trip.

I quickly downed a couple vodka shots to try to catch up with him. An hour later, we stumbled the few blocks' walk to Calumet. After just one dance, I went to the bar for a vodka lemonade, and when I returned, Andy was nowhere to be found. Panicked that I may have seen him for the last time, I stepped outside and dialed his number. He answered on the third ring.

"Katie!"

"Where are you? Did you leave?" I asked, trying to hide the urgency I felt.

"Parpetsi," he muttered, naming the street around the

corner from Calumet that led to his apartment. "Going home."

"Do you want some company?"

"Sure."

I hung up the phone and walked to the corner of Pushkin and Parpetsi as quickly as I could, wary of drawing attention to myself but not wanting to lose the chance to catch up with Andy. As soon as I turned onto Parpetsi and out of the view of anyone hanging outside of Calumet, my walk turned into a sprint. After just two blocks, I saw a solitary figure walking slowly down the middle of the sidewalk just ahead of me. I didn't waste one second before running up beside him and throwing my arm around his shoulder.

He slipped his arm around my waist, hand on my hip, and gave me a quick kiss. As we walked back to his Soviet-era apartment building, the bottom of my shirt rode up my back, and I could feel his warm hand on my bare skin. We stumbled through the dark entryway of his building as every move we made seemed to echo. An open elevator was waiting for us, and as the door slammed shut, Andy pulled me around so that we were face to face, nose to nose, and soon, lips to lips.

Once inside the apartment, we stood in his moonlit living room and kissed again until he suddenly pulled away. My mind was racing. Had he changed his mind? Did he regret bringing me home? Without a word, he made a beeline for the small bathroom just off the living room. I heard a click as he locked the door behind him. It wasn't long before I heard the too-familiar sound of someone's entire dinner erupting into the toilet.

Five minutes soon became 15 minutes. I knocked on the door, at first a gentle tap but soon with more force. When he didn't respond, I called out his name, not so quietly that he couldn't hear me but not so loudly that a neighbor would worry. Still, nothing. I jiggled the door handle, but the locked door wouldn't budge. Not wanting to disappear on him and even holding out some hope that he might emerge from the bathroom feeling better, I took off my sandals, lay down on his full-size bed, and passed out.

I awoke to the sound of Andy snoring next to me. He was out cold. A wave of embarrassment washed over me. What was I doing there? Would he even remember me walking home with him? How would he react if he woke up with me in his bed? And what would my poor host parents think about me walking in the door at sunrise? I quietly slipped on my sandals, grabbed my purse and tiptoed out, taking care not to let the heavy door slam on my way out.

* * *

Tears welled in my eyes as I walked across the bridge leading to Georgia just over 24 hours later, an exit stamp from Armenia fresh in my passport. For the first time in more than seven months on the road, I longed to stay somewhere. While I would later write a blog post talking about how much Armenia meant to me and the lessons I learned there, in that moment, the tears were only for Andy and what might have been. I really liked him.

My last day and night in Yerevan had been anticlimactic. A day-long group bicycle excursion in unseasonably hot temperatures to Echmiadzin Cathedral 20 kilometers away left me dehydrated and sunburned. Stolen conversations with Andy during the trip confirmed his memory of our encounter was hazy at best; he recalled me being at his apartment but admitted he had no idea how I got there. I conveniently left out the part about me inviting myself over. That night, while everyone gathered at one of our favorite pubs to bid me farewell, Andy was the last to arrive, two hours late. I couldn't enjoy myself; I was too distracted by the thought that I might not get to say goodbye. A couple bars and several drinks later, it was all over. Our group of more than a dozen had shrunk to six when everyone decided to call it a night. Before I could even process what was happening, Andy was hugging me goodbye and then getting into a taxi with Jeff and riding away.

As I got back into the marshrutka taking me to Tbilisi, I replayed not only the previous night but the past few weeks in my head, wondering if, once again, I misread a guy's intentions and felt a connection where there really was none. The buzz of my Blackberry interrupted my thoughts, and I looked down to see a text from Andy:

"Safe travels! We'll hold down the fort until you return. See you soon."

I couldn't wait to return.

10
Turkey & Georgia (Again)

I sat in a mostly empty cafe on Istanbul's Galata Bridge as a waiter approached me with a smile, throwing out a jumble of words in Turkish.

"Can I please get a menu?" I asked slowly, hoping he would speak English.

"Oh, are you a tourist?" he replied perfectly.

"Yes," I replied with a chuckle, wondering how he could possibly think this blonde woman sitting in front of him was anything but a tourist.

"Sorry I was speaking Turkish to you," he responded. "I thought you were Turkish."

And thus began my month-long detour in Turkey.

Thanks to the Black Sea ferry delay, I hadn't obtained my visa to Azerbaijan as planned. This meant my carefully curated itinerary was suddenly up in the air. So after leaving Armenia, I stopped in Tbilisi for a night before flying to Rome for a travel blogging conference in Tuscany. I thought a detour would provide a much-needed diversion from Andy and the opportunity to meet many of my new online friends in person for the first time. While I had drifted from many of my friends in Chicago, I had developed new friendships online with fellow long-term travelers and travel bloggers. Finally connecting with them in person and traveling around Italy together provided a great emotional boost. I was thrilled to learn that several of my new friends would also be moving on to Istanbul after the conference.

Istanbul was a shock to the system. After almost eight months of traveling far away from any tourist hot spots, I forgot what it was like to push through crowds and to hear American and Australian accents at every turn. I forgot the feeling of annoyance as touts competed for my attention, hissing "hey lady" and "yes, please"—even following me down the street to cajole me into visiting their shops. I forgot that the simple act of asking someone for directions could lead to someone trying to sell me a scarf or carpet or spices.

While I had spent months staying in nearly empty hostels, my hostel in Istanbul's historic district of Sultanahmet was nearly sold out, packed full of Aussies and Kiwis in Turkey for ANZAC Day. Walking through the streets of the old city, my frustration grew steadily as I got stuck behind meandering tourists or groups of Turkish teenagers blocking the narrow sidewalks. I did my best to stare straight ahead and not react as tout after tout leaned into me, insisting I check out their restaurant or carpet shop. I was beginning to remember why I enjoyed getting off the beaten path so much.

At the same time, it was nice to be somewhere where nearly everyone spoke at least some English, something I hadn't enjoyed since I left Chicago. The tourist infrastructure was excellent, with numerous public toilets, frequent signage and tourist information booths. My hostel was far more than a large flat in an old building; it was a four-story, stand-alone structure with a large kitchen, multiple common areas and, best of all, a rooftop bar and restaurant that overlooked the old city.

After my late lunch of chicken kebabs, salad and a delicate glass of Turkish tea, I met up with some other bloggers for a walking tour of Istanbul. The group was refreshingly small—just four of us—and our guide, Suzan, boasted an impressive resume with a background in Ottoman and modern Turkish scholarship. Suzan led us along the port to a well-known baklava spot, Karaköy Güllüoğlu. As someone who is gluten-intolerant, I wasn't initially thrilled with a stop for baklava, a Turkish pastry made from phyllo dough. But not only did Suzan inform me they had gluten-free baklava, she ordered gluten-free for everyone. I was shocked and grateful. It was the first time on my trip that someone really tried to cater to my special dietary needs.

From there, Suzan led us through the Karaköy, Beyoglu and Galata neighborhoods. We walked down streets that no tour would've included a decade earlier but were now lined with shops and cafes, a sign of gentrification. We passed a Turkish Orthodox church, an Armenian church and a former Russian Orthodox church that looked like any other apartment building before stopping at a 16th century mosque that resembled a smaller version of the famous Aya Sophia. Suzan explained the protocol to follow when entering the mosque, including removing our shoes, covering our heads, and putting on robes to cover our "tight" jeans.

The next night, I was back on Istiklal Street to meet up

with an even larger group of bloggers at a traditional Turkish meze restaurant. It was a mix of those who had been in Italy with me, a few who had been on the tour the previous night and a Turkish blogger named Ahmet, who I was meeting in person for the first time. A mutual friend, Rob, had introduced us by email weeks earlier as I tried to plan my time in Turkey.

As dinner progressed, Ahmet started grilling me. How long had I known Rob? How did we meet? What did I think of him? For a split second, I wondered if Ahmet was trying to figure out if Rob and I were dating, but I quickly pushed the thought from my mind. After dinner, we ended up walking far ahead of the rest of the group. As we reached Taksim Square, Ahmet hailed a taxi for me, but not before asking if I wanted to hang out again before I left Istanbul. He immediately added, "no pressure, no pressure." As my taxi sped away toward my hostel, I wondered if I had just been asked on a date.

I spent the next couple of days learning about the Ottoman Empire, exploring Istanbul's massive spice bazaar and taking a cruise on the Bosphorus. I met up with Ahmet for dinner on my last night in the city, not sure at all what to expect. Despite our cultural differences, we shared a love of travel and the conversation at a Turkish fast-food restaurant flowed easily for more than two hours. Ahmet wanted to show me more of Istanbul, so we wandered down Istiklal Street, trying oysters from a street vendor before popping into a bar with a band playing Turkish folk music. We danced to a few songs and then moved on to a packed karaoke club. If I was back home, I would've sworn I was on a great first date. As we stood shoulder to shoulder at the bar, Ahmet bemoaned the fact that I was leaving to go to Amasya the next day. He begged me to stay just a few more days as I swooned over the way he said "Amasya" in his Turkish accent. The next thing I knew, he had his arm around me and pulled me in for a kiss. By the time we returned to his flat a few blocks away, the sun was coming up.

As I hugged Ahmet goodbye, I felt nothing like I did after bidding farewell to Andy. My encounter with Ahmet was spontaneous and unexpected, and I didn't have time to develop an emotional connection. I sent him a nice message before I boarded my overnight bus to Amasya but didn't think too much about if or when I might see him again. To be honest, it was refreshing to feel that way. To be able to enjoy a night out with Ahmet that was nothing more than a fun night out without any expectations was both a relief and a confidence boost.

* * *

My eyes squinted as I stepped up into the unknown. It was impossible to see my next move in the dark, so I simply had to trust and follow the steps of the man in front of me. Despite a sign saying it was off-limits, I was climbing the minaret of an 11th century mosque, said to be the first mosque built by an early Turkish empire in the ancient Armenian capital of Ani. But I wasn't in Armenia; I was in modern-day Turkey, exploring what remained of what was once a magnificent city on the banks of the Akhuryan River. The city had once rivaled Baghdad, Cairo, and Istanbul in splendor and prominence, but it had lain in ruins for nearly a century. The man in front of me was a security guard named Orhan.

After leaving Istanbul, I spent a few days in the cute city of Amasya before moving on to Trabzon along the Black Sea coast. I made an overnight stop in the very conservative city of Erzurum before continuing to Kars in far eastern Turkey for the sole purpose of taking a day trip to Ani. Not accessible by public transport, I hired a driver through my hotel. We drove for an hour from Kars to reach the entrance to Ani. Once inside, I explored using a map in my guidebook and relying on explanatory plaques near the major buildings to fill in the gaps. I was the only person there.

Once known as "the city of a thousand and one churches," Ani became the capital of the Armenian kingdom in the middle of the 10th century and grew to more than 100,000 inhabitants. But after centuries of invasions and sieges, it was completely abandoned by the 1700s. Ani experienced a resurgence in the 19th century only to be closed off for good after World War I and the Armenian Genocide of 1918. When I visited, what remained of the capital stood in eastern Turkey, separated from Armenia only by the Akhuryan River flowing below it. Due to its location on the border, permits were required to visit as recently as 2004 and photography was prohibited. By 2012, though, authorities had relaxed these restrictions and Ani was open to visitors.

Ani was like an open-air museum, but unlike many museums that consist of reconstructed buildings, the ruins of Ani sat untouched. Some buildings still stood tall, while others lay in ruins, the victims of gradual deterioration or the occasional earthquake. In the case of one church, a lightning strike in 1957 destroyed half the building, leaving an open shell surrounded by piles of crumbled stones. Given the historic conflict between the Turks and the Armenians, and Ani's location just inside the border, what remained of the city was left to disintegrate.

What I saw there was a poignant reminder of what was once a great capital city. I stood in awe of the colorful frescoes in the Church of St. Gregory the Illuminator, the only ones that survived in Ani. I wandered through a maze of 12th century homes and climbed and crawled over the debris of the rotunda of a different Church of St. Gregory that collapsed as soon as it was finished. And I stared in amazement at the open ceiling of the 10th century cathedral that was later converted into a mosque after the Turks conquered Ani.

I thought I had the ruins all to myself, but then Orhan appeared, wearing the uniform of a security guard. I was cautious at first; he didn't speak much English, and with no one else in sight, I wasn't quite sure what he wanted. But his smile seemed genuine, and I couldn't say no when he offered to take my picture in front of a church and a caravanserai and the city walls. As a solo traveler in the days before selfie sticks, I rarely got pictures of myself. As Orhan beckoned me to follow him to the base of the minaret, I knew I had a unique opportunity. I quickly shook off my fears that climbing the ancient structure may not be safe. When we reached the top of the forbidden tower, I was able to see for miles around. When I faced east, I could see right over the river into Armenia—so close, yet so far away.

* * *

I stared out of the dusty back window of the black clunker that had carried me less than a mile from the Turkey-Georgia border to a gas station in the middle of nowhere. The large Turkish man, I'll call him Berat, who had been at my side for the last few hours, was arguing heatedly with the driver of the car, a sly-looking Georgian man with a red mustache. As they battled it out, the older Turkish gentleman, I'll call him Omer, who completed our traveling trio, stood fuming by the trunk of the car. I expected him to grab his things and storm off in anger at any moment. All I could do was sit frozen in the back seat, my mind racing. What had I gotten myself into? And what could I do to get myself out of this situation and on my way to Tbilisi?

My day had begun in Turkey more than five hours earlier. After three weeks of smooth travel through the country, almost nothing went as planned as I tried to leave. I arrived at the bus station in the center of Kars shortly before 8 a.m. to buy a ticket to nearby Ardahan. There, I was supposed to catch a bus coming from Istanbul that would take me across the border to the town of Akhaltsikhe in Georgia. This was one of two routes suggested by my guidebook. The other was to take a minibus to a town 12 kilometers from the border called Posof, a taxi from Posof to the border, and another taxi from the border to Akhaltsikhe. There, I would find regular marshrutkas to Tbilisi.

All indications were that the connection would be tight. To help ensure things went smoothly, I had a note in Turkish explaining to the minibus driver to take me all the way to the *otogar* in Ardahan to catch the bus. As I showed this note to the driver, he smiled and nodded, which I found reassuring. Indeed, we rolled into Ardahan half an hour before the bus from Istanbul was scheduled to arrive. I walked confidently into the small ticket office, followed by a bulky Turkish man who appeared to be in his early forties—that would be Berat—and a mustachioed, gray-haired gentleman in a tweed blazer—Omer.

"You going Tbilisi?" Berat asked me as he pointed to himself and Omer, which I interpreted to mean they were going there as well.

I slowly nodded, not sure how to respond. I thought the bus I was waiting for only went as far as Akhaltsikhe, about one hour from the border and three hours from Tbilisi. I tried to confirm with the clerk behind the counter when a white-haired man standing nearby took out what looked like a ticket pad, started writing on it, and asked to see my passport. Since I would be crossing a border, I didn't think anything of that—when going from Yerevan to Tbilisi, the driver collected our passports in advance. But this man gave my passport back to me almost immediately. Suddenly Berat was trying to convince me to take a taxi to Posof with him and Omer instead of the bus. I spoke no Turkish, and they spoke little English, but after a lot of back and forth and pointing at maps, everyone in the ticket office convinced me that, for some mysterious reason, there was no bus to Akhaltsikhe after all. My only option would be to wait almost two hours for the next minibus to Posof, or I could share a taxi to Posof with Berat and Omer. I reluctantly chose the latter.

While Berat initially quoted me 50 Turkish lira (about $28) for my share of the taxi, I got him down to 30 lira

($17). I was sure I was overpaying, but after our harrowing hour-long ride to Posof, I saw both men contribute 30 lira to the driver as well, making me feel slightly better. Not really knowing what to do or where to go, I followed Berat and Omer when we arrived in Posof. Berat seemed to know his way around, calling out to a guy named Ismail, who happened to be driving a white minibus. After sitting Omer and me down in yet another small ticket office while he went to get lunch, Berat returned with Ismail, who told me it would be $20 to go to Tbilisi. This seemed reasonable, and after confirming multiple times that he would indeed take me all the way to Tbilisi, I agreed and handed over the cash in US dollars. Within minutes, I was sprawled out in the backseat of Ismail's minibus, thinking I was set.

I should have known something was up when we had to take all our belongings out of the minibus at the border. On prior border crossings, I'd left my bags on the marshrutka or bus. Berat insisted on carrying my large backpack as we entered the immigration building. I was relieved to not have to carry it, but also annoyed because I didn't trust him. My anxiety rose as a newbie border guard questioned me as I tried to enter Georgia for the third time in three months while another guard waved Berat through with my pack. Soon, he was out of my sight. When I finally emerged from the immigration office, I saw Berat and Omer standing next to an old black sedan, my backpack in the trunk, and the minibus nowhere to be seen. I suddenly felt sick to my stomach, but what choice did I have but to get in the car?

Berat and Omer began arguing in Turkish as soon as the car doors slammed shut. I could make out "dollar," "lari," and "kilometer." Were they fighting over the fare? Suddenly, we pulled off the road into a gas station parking lot, and Omer jumped out of the front seat. Berat soon followed, and after a heated exchange between the two of them, the driver hopped out and inserted himself in the argument. Up until this point, I'd thought Berat and Omer knew each other and were traveling together. As I watched them argue, I realized that Omer was just along for the ride and was as frustrated as I was—likely more so because he understood exactly what was happening. I don't know what was said as I sat staring out of the dirty car window, but eventually, Berat convinced Omer to get back in the car and we continued.

At that point, I went on the offensive. I was already in deeper than I probably should have been. While I didn't feel physically in danger, I did feel like I had been naive about Berat's intentions. I was mad at myself for being where I was. At the same time, there was no way I was handing over another dime to anyone for this journey. We were now in Georgia, and I knew that most Georgians who grew up in Soviet times spoke Russian. I guessed that was the case with the driver. Berat's jaw dropped as I started a conversation with him.

"*Ya ne znayu etikh muzhchin. Ya zaplatil im 20 dollarov, chtoby oni poyekhali v Tbilisi,*" I said quietly as I leaned toward the driver from the backseat. "*Ya ne khochu platit' bol'she.*"

I explained to him that I had already paid to go all the way to Tbilisi and that I was not paying anymore. Knowing what I knew of Georgians and Georgian hospitality, I suspected that if he knew my situation, he would likely sympathize with me. I was right.

"*Da, ya ponimayu. Vse normal'no.*" He nodded and assured me everything was fine. "*Ty moya sestra, ya pozabochus' o tebe.*"

I smiled as he told me I was like his sister and that he would take care of me. My whole body relaxed as I was suddenly confident that all would be okay. To my surprise, I had also opened a can of worms with a driver eager to understand American politics. It was a presidential election year back home, but I had managed to avoid any conversation about it on my travels to that point. I was also blissfully unaware of the primary campaigns that were underway. The driver, however, was keen to discuss the merits of Mitt Romney and whether his election would help Georgia gain membership in NATO. I was relieved that it wasn't long before we pulled into the bus station in Akhaltsikhe.

The driver showed us where the marshrutka to Tbilisi departed, and then Berat pointed out to me that there was a currency exchange—I still needed to change my lira for Georgian lari. As I waited my turn at the currency exchange window, Berat stuck to me like glue, barely giving me room to breathe. I tried to push him away and shielded my lira as I handed them over to the guy behind the glass. I suspected Berat wanted to see how much money I was changing. Sure enough, as the clerk handed lari back to me, Berat hovered right over my shoulder, obviously wanting to see how much cash I had on me. I glared at him and stormed off, trying to hide the cash from him as best I could.

I returned to the marshrutka and learned from the driver that the fare was 20 lari—about $12. Berat appeared a few minutes later and, although I knew he didn't understand Russian, I told him in Russian right in front of the marshrutka driver that because I had already paid him to go to Tbilisi, he needed to pay for my minibus ticket. He scowled at me, then looked at the driver, who held out his hand, asking for the money. Berat glared back at me, defeated, and motioned to me to get on the bus as he covered the fare. Although we were forced to sit next to each other for the entire ride, Berat didn't speak to me again.

By the time we arrived in Tbilisi, the disappointment I'd felt in myself for getting into such a sticky situation was replaced by a sense of satisfaction. I was proud of how I handled things and could feel my confidence continue to grow.

* * *

Days after arriving in Tbilisi, I headed to Mestia, a village in the Svaneti region of Georgia. It was high up in the mountains, not far from the border with Russia. Svaneti was home to a culture that had existed in Georgia since the second millennium B.C. and a people who spoke an ancient dialect of Georgian that most others in the country couldn't really understand. The region also provided the best hiking opportunities in the Caucasus. While I hardly ever went hiking at home, I found myself seeking out occasions to hike as I traveled.

With only one full day in Mestia, I decided to hike to the top of Mount Mestia, about a five hour round trip. Following vague instructions in my guidebook, I set out from the center of the village under dark gray skies. A narrow road led me past a few homes and historic Svan towers. After passing under a crumbling brick arch, the road turned into a footpath. According to my guidebook, the footpath would lead to a jeep trail that I could follow to the top. When no jeep trail appeared after a few minutes, though, I began to question whether I should continue. I wasn't a regular hiker and had even less experience hiking solo. Should I really be attempting a five-hour hike in an unfamiliar place by myself? The confidence I gained on my journey from Kars to Tbilisi was suddenly missing.

I reluctantly kept going. Soon, I spotted two wide lines of paint on a rock – one orange and one white. While my guidebook didn't mention the trail markings, I remembered that a woman in Mestia's small tourist office had told me that orange and white markers would show the way up to the cross. Suddenly, I knew I was headed in the right direction. The trail ended up being very well marked. The one time I was genuinely confused, I turned back as soon as I realized I hadn't seen any markers in a few minutes. Sure enough, I saw them almost immediately after retracing my steps, leading up a path I hadn't noticed earlier.

The hike was challenging. While I had started running again in Yerevan and had continued the workouts I started in Kyiv, I was still not in great shape. I was certainly not in the shape I was when I ran a personal best in the Tallinn Marathon eight months earlier. It was also my first real hike since a subzero adventure through deep snow in a Siberian nature reserve back in November. Luckily, the trail was well-maintained, with little loose rock or slippery spots. Aside from the occasional cows and shepherd dogs, I had the path to myself. I relished the solitude.

As the cross at the top of Mount Mestia came into view, the sound of laughter broke the silence. I was no longer alone; I was sharing the mountain top with a half dozen teenage boys. Even though I was more than twice their age—and an age at which I shouldn't care what a group of teenage boys think of me—I could feel my entire body tense up as I looked around for a spot to sit. All I wanted to do was rest and enjoy the view and a Snickers bar, but now I was too self-conscious to do so. There was something about being around a group of boys that age that brought me right back to my adolescence. Just like my acne scars that never quite faded, the cackling sound of others joking at my expense never went away. I may have been standing on the top of a mountain in a foreign country, but in my head, I was back in White Bear Lake, the laughter of these boys aimed squarely at me. Never mind that they barely seemed to realize I was there.

The feeling of raindrops falling on my forehead interrupted my thoughts. I quickly shoved my half-eaten Snickers into my pack and dug out my umbrella. As I hurried down the way I came, I was relieved to be on my own again. The path seemed so obvious, and I was in such a rush to get as far as possible before the drizzle turned into a downpour, that I lost sight of the white and orange markers that I followed on the way up. After about 40 minutes, I stared down below me and realized I couldn't see the telltale Svan towers in Mestia down below. While I thought I had been crisscrossing down the mountain, I was heading far out of town.

At first, I continued slowly along the same path, thinking a turn must be coming that would take me back in the right direction. Then I thought I would just continue to the bottom and follow the riverbank back to Mestia. But as I strained to look at the river, I wasn't confident that a path or road existed that would take me all the way back. As the wind picked up and the rain started hitting me sideways, I reluctantly decided to turn around and retrace my steps until I found where I went wrong. Thankfully, it wasn't long before I saw a path that I previously missed. It seemed to cut straight across the mountain back to Mestia, but I didn't see any markers to reassure me.

I shrugged and said out loud "why the hell not?" If I had learned anything on my trip so far, it was to trust my instincts. The path went up and down but continued in the right direction and eventually led me to the outskirts of Mestia. I made my way through a small village and soon emerged on a paved road taking me straight to the center of town. With my shoes caked in mud and the rest of me soaked from the rain, I stumbled into the first café I saw and ordered a double plate of shashlik (Georgian barbecue) and a huge plate of fries. My presence was met by uncomfortable stares, but I was too tired and hungry to care. I was just relieved to be safely back in Mestia.

* * *

Getting safely back to Tbilisi would be another story. I left Mestia around 6 a.m. The sun was already shining brightly, but the mountain air was chilly enough that I wore my windbreaker. When the marshrutka picked me up at 5:30, I felt lucky to secure the last remaining single seat on the right-hand side of the van—no smelly drunk men falling asleep and drooling on my shoulder as there had been on my ride up to Mestia. This group seemed to be a calm mix of professional-looking Georgians, including several well-dressed women in heels and full makeup.

The three-hour ride to Mestia from Zugdidi a few days earlier had been nerve-wracking, but not terrifying—probably because we were going up, which necessarily made for slower going. This time, though, the driver seemed to be on a mission to get down the mountain as fast as possible, barely slowing down as he whipped around one hairpin turn after another. Within 30 minutes of departing Mestia, we made our first stop. While I had heard stories of frequent stops on these trips for drinking, eating and more drinking, this was just the opposite—a woman sitting in the back was already green from motion sickness. About an hour later, we stopped again. And just past Zugdidi, we stopped yet again. It all made me very glad I did not eat breakfast before we left.

While I thankfully didn't succumb to motion sickness, I was trying to hold on for dear life. My single seat that I thought was perfect turned out to be a disaster. With no seatbelt, I spent the ride holding on to a small piece of rubber lining the window to keep myself from sliding off the seat at every turn. Add in a slightly awkward angle of the seat and words don't do justice to how much the left side of my butt hurt by the time we arrived in Tbilisi. When the marshrutka finally pulled into the parking lot of the main train station in Tbilisi, I was able to breathe for the first time in about eight hours.

* * *

Thanks to my quirky itinerary and closed borders between

Armenia and Turkey, and Armenia and Azerbaijan, I would end up visiting Georgia five times on my trip. It was only on the third visit that I took time to explore the country that ended up being one of my favorites. After my weekend trip to Mestia, I based myself in Tbilisi for a few days. When I wasn't strolling along tree-lined Rustaveli Avenue or relaxing at Prospero's Books, I was wandering through the narrow streets of the Old Town past centuries-old churches and colorful homes with decorative balconies. I also took a few days to take day trips outside of Tbilisi, visiting Stalin's birthplace in the city of Gori, the former Georgian capital of Mtskheta, the cave city of Uplistsikhe and the cave monastery of Davit Gareja.

As I prepared to move on to Azerbaijan, I booked a couple nights at a bed and breakfast in the city of Telavi in the Kakheti region of Georgia. Georgia was the second country (after Armenia) to officially adopt Christianity as its religion back in the 4th century and archaeologists have traced the origins of wine production in the country to 6,000 B.C. in Georgia. Kakheti was home to a plethora of monasteries and wineries, providing a great overview of the country's religious history and its wine-making tradition. I hired a driver for two days to see as much as possible before it was time for me to move on to my final stop in the Caucasus: Azerbaijan.

11
Azerbaijan

"*Devushka!*"

I was walking along the side of the road in Telavi on my way to the bus station—basically a large parking lot with a single ticket window. I hoped to catch an 8:45 a.m. marshrutka to the town of Lagodekhi near the Georgia-Azerbaijan border. I barely realized that the voice was calling to me when I heard it again with more urgency.

"*De-vush-ka!*"

I looked up to see the driver of a large bus waving out his window at me.

"Lagodekhi?" He asked me once he saw he had my attention.

"*Da!*" I yelled back and hurried across the busy street to board this enormous bus as one of only three passengers. After I took my seat next to a stocky Georgian guy who seemed to be selling tickets, he asked if I was going to Azerbaijan. When I replied in the affirmative, he informed me the bus was going all the way to Balaken—the nearest border town on the Azeri side. So instead of hiring a taxi from Lagodekhi to the border and another taxi from the border to Balaken, I was now set to go straight through—all for just seven lari—about four dollars.

A week earlier, I had arranged for my visa to Azerbaijan using a travel company in Tbilisi that I found in a Lonely Planet forum. I sent the company my completed visa application by email, together with a scan of my passport. Then, the morning after I arrived back in Tbilisi from Mestia, I found the company's unremarkable office in a small alley about a mile from Tbilisi's Old Town. I handed my passport to a heavy, brassy-haired woman who appeared to be in her late forties or fifties. When I returned eight hours later, I placed $140 in crisp 20-dollar bills on the desk in front of the same woman. After counting my bills, she handed my passport back to me without saying a word. Not wanting her to think I didn't trust her, I waited until I was outside to open my increasingly full passport. My heart sank when I saw the Azeri visa. My name and the dates of my stay were written in block letters by hand. It didn't even look real. Had I been scammed? The possibility of a fake Azeri visa only added to my anxiety about crossing the border into Azerbaijan.

Most of my anxiety stemmed from the fact that I had an Armenian visa in my passport. The history of conflict between Armenia and Azerbaijan went back nearly a century, to the Armenian-Azerbaijani War fought over three contested regions from 1918 to 1920. More recently, in the late 1980s and early 1990s, the two countries again engaged in an armed conflict over Nagorno-Karabakh (known to Armenians as Artsakh), an enclave of Azerbaijan with a majority Armenian population. Known as the Nagorno-Karabakh

War, a ceasefire was proclaimed in 1994, but tensions still ran high (indeed, just a few days after I made my journey to Azerbaijan, Azeri troops shot and killed three Armenian soldiers near the border). The possibility that Azerbaijan might not let me in after I visited Armenia seemed very real. I'd even taken the precaution of hiding all the files on my computer related to Armenia and deleting all the Armenian last names on my Blackberry. If the border guards searched my belongings, I didn't want to give them any reason to prevent me from crossing into Azerbaijan or, even worse, detain me.

"Go to Tbilisi and get a second passport. That's the only way they'll let you in," warned my guide in Kars.

"No way you'll get in," claimed David as I explained my plans to visit Azerbaijan shortly after we met during my volunteer stint in Armenia.

"Oooh, if you have Armenia in your passport, I don't know if that'll happen," warned fellow volunteer Shirak as we exchanged instant messages just an hour before I departed Telavi for the border.

"Good luck," offered a large blue and white sign as the bus approached the Georgia-Azerbaijan border. At least the Georgians had a sense of humor, I thought, laughing to myself.

We reached the border promptly at 10 a.m. Leaving my belongings on the bus, I followed two Azeri women through the immigration checkpoint to exit Georgia. After clearing that easily, we climbed back on the bus to head toward Azerbaijan. After waiting behind a short line of cars, several heavily armed guards waved us through. A couple hundred meters later, the bus driver told me to leave the bus and take all my luggage with me. An Azeri guard pointed me to a narrow walkway, which would presumably take me to the immigration checkpoint to enter Azerbaijan. The guard gave me a smile as he pointed me the way—something I tried to tell myself was a good sign. I walked far ahead of the two older women and was alone when I reached a metal door leading to the immigration desk.

A chubby guard with a buzz cut greeted me with a "hello" in English. He then took the passport from my outstretched hand and sat down behind a computer and glass window as I waited. I had opened it to the page with my Azeri visa, hoping he wouldn't look any further. But I had no such luck—he flipped through the entire document, pausing twice at the sight of my Armenian visa.

"You have been to Armenia?"

"Yes, I have been to Armenia."

I thought of adding that I had not been to Nagorno-Karabakh, a visit which would automatically deny me entry to Azerbaijan. But I didn't want to give him any ideas.

"One minute," the guard stated as he walked into a back room with my passport. I tapped my fingers nervously on the counter as I listened to an indecipherable exchange between the guard and an unseen woman in the back.

My mind drifted back to my only other challenging border crossing: going from Moldova to Ukraine. When I made that trip two months earlier, I sat quietly in the second row of a marshrutka as the driver collected passports from everyone on board and handed them off to the Ukrainian immigration officers waiting outside. A few minutes later, he stepped back into the van and pointed to me.

"You! American! Come!" I followed the driver into a small wooden building, where I was greeted by a blonde woman in uniform sitting next to a computer.

"*Vy govorite po-russki?*"

"*Da,*" I tried to respond with confidence.

Soon, she peppered me with questions in Russian: where was I coming from [Chisinau], where was I going [Odesa], what would I be doing in Ukraine, where would I go next, and how would I get there?

And this was where we got stuck. I could not remember the Russian word for boat or ship, so I struggled to explain that I would be going from Odesa to Georgia by boat—I would be taking a ferry across the Black Sea. After several minutes of back and forth and a second officer jumping into the conversation, the marshrutka driver interjected in English. He quickly helped me explain that I was taking the ferry, but this revelation only led to more questions about the boat itself, none of which I could answer. Suddenly, the officers gave up. All was good. I could leave. Their lightheartedness in letting me go so quickly was a stark contrast to the situation in front of me.

After what felt like an eternity, the Azeri officer returned, not saying a word but wearing a stern frown on his face. He scanned my passport, opened it up to the page with my Azeri visa, and started slowly entering the information into the computer, punching every key with force.

Minutes later, he grabbed what I'd been waiting for—the stamp to officially grant me entry into Azerbaijan. He gruffly handed back my passport and waved me through to the next room, which held a large X-ray machine and a metal detector. He clearly didn't want to let me into the country, but the invisible woman in the back office must have told him he had to. As far as I could tell, he didn't inform the guards in that room about my unpalatable Armenian visa. They greeted me with a smile. My bags rolled through the X-ray machine untouched and unexamined, and I walked through the metal detector with ease. As I collected my things, I looked at the guard sitting next to the X-ray video screen and asked, "*Khorosho?*"

He nodded. "Enjoy your stay."

From the border, I continued on the same bus to the town of Balaken. There, I caught another bus to the town of Qax (pronounced "Gakh"), where I met Sevinj, the local manager for Community Based Tourism Azerbaijan (CBT). CBT was a fledgling organization founded by a former Peace Corps volunteer that aimed to show visitors the "real" Azerbaijan by connecting them with local families while also financially benefiting the local communities. It had a growing network of homestays around the country and working with them saved me the trouble of trying to find places to stay on my own. Hostels didn't really exist in Azerbaijan outside of Baku at that time (and even in Baku, there were few), so staying with local families was also the least expensive option for accommodation. Assistance from the local managers once I arrived was a huge plus as well.

I was relieved to find Sevinj at the station waiting for me when I stepped off the bus in Qax. She accompanied me in a taxi to my host family in the nearby village of Lekit. There, we sat down to tea with the family and discussed the details of my stay—whether I wanted to add lunch and/or dinner (breakfast was included), whether I wanted to use any guiding services, and the logistics for my departure two days later. My host "parents" spoke only Azeri and some Russian, and their teenage son, Turan, spoke just a little English. We communicated through hand gestures and facial expressions—mostly smiles. The living conditions were about what I expected. I had a comfortable twin bed in my own room in the house and the toilet was a flushable squat toilet in an outhouse out back. The shower was inside the house, but the water had to be heated by a wood stove before using it, which took nearly an hour.

Sevinj gave me a tour of Qax the next morning. The city of Qax was the capital of the region with the same name. Like so many other places I'd visit on this trip, the area had ancient roots, with settlements dating back to the Bronze and Iron Ages. We walked around the old quarter surrounded by thick stone walls that had been restored more than a century earlier. Sevinj also showed me around the Qax History Museum, adding context to the displays of tools, weapons and national costumes. Of the surrounding villages we visited, Ilisu was my favorite, with a series of quaint stone buildings set in a green mountain valley.

In the afternoon, Turan took me hiking around Lekit to see some ruined Albanian churches and the Mamirli ("green moss") waterfall. I was confused to learn that the Albanian churches had no connection to the country of Albania in Europe. They were instead remnants of an ancient civilization that once called modern-day Azerbaijan home. As we hiked, Turan seemed to always be several steps ahead of me, easily scaling fences and running full speed down trails covered with loose rocks and tree roots. Every time he escaped from my line of sight, I called out in both Russian and English, pleading with him to stop and wait for me. Rather than slow down, he seemed to pick up the pace. Was he trying to lose me? If I had any idea how to get back home, I wouldn't have minded. But without a map or phone number for my host family, the thought of getting lost in the woods in Azerbaijan terrified me.

My legs wobbled like jelly by the time we emerged from the woods. I could picture my cozy bed and I longed for a nap. But Turan had other ideas. After a short conversation with his mother in Azeri, he said we were going to his uncle's house for dinner. I half-heartedly smiled, trying not to give away the fact that all I wanted to do was sleep. Not wanting to be rude, I summoned all my energy to follow Turan across the vast grassy field that separated my homestay from Turan's uncle.

The house was deceptively far away and we had no clear trail to follow. After nearly an hour, the tall grass gave way to scattered trees and I could see a house in the distance. Turan's aunt and uncle were waiting for us out front. As I stared ahead, though, I didn't notice a change in the terrain. Before I realized what was happening, my right leg was buried in mud up to my knee. I screamed as my arms flailed, trying to keep my balance so I wouldn't completely topple over.

I was in too deep, and the mud was too thick for me to pull myself out. Turan seemed indifferent to my plight, but his uncle saw what happened and came rushing toward me, quickly extending both hands to help lift me from the mud. My mud-caked jeans clung to my leg as I limped toward their home. I could feel the sludge squish between my toes with every step. When I reached the front door, Turan's aunt motioned for me to remove my shoes and handed me a pair of slightly too-large Croc-like sandals to slip on instead. Turan's uncle soon appeared with a large bucket of water to rinse off my jeans, although it probably would've been more efficient to strip them off altogether.

After cleaning up, Turan's aunt invited me inside for a cup of tea. But I was searching for Turan, wanting to ask him if we could return home. As much as I appreciated his aunt's and uncle's hospitality, I just needed to leave. It wasn't the first time I'd felt like that on my trip, and it wouldn't be the last. It was one of the consequences of traveling as an introvert. As much as I enjoyed meeting new people and talking with strangers, it sucked the energy out of me. I would get to a point where I just needed some time to myself to relax and recharge. I wish I'd realized and embraced this about myself earlier in life, as I spent years forcing myself out into social situations when I really didn't have the energy to positively interact with people. I can recall so many Friday and Saturday nights in my 20s when I forced myself to meet friends at a bar or party because it just wasn't "cool" to be sitting home alone on a weekend night.

By the time I stayed with Turan and his family, I'd spent most of my trip living with other people, from homestays in Russia, Ukraine, and Armenia to hostels in the Baltics and Georgia. I shied away from Couchsurfing, which was increasing in popularity in 2012, because I didn't want to come home from a long day of sightseeing and feel compelled to socialize with my host. Yet I signed up for homestays in the interest of both cultural immersion and my tight budget. When I fell into the mudhole near Turan's uncle's home, I hit a cumulative breaking point. All I could think about was returning to the homestay, crawling into bed and falling asleep. Eventually, Turan's uncle agreed to give me a ride back to my homestay. Turan's aunt was clearly disappointed that I wasn't staying for dinner after all. As the car pulled out of the driveway, I felt ashamed, realizing I'd likely offended them. I wish I knew how to adequately explain how I felt, but the overwhelming desire to be alone was something I could rarely explain in English, much less in Russian.

* * *

"You have sex with me," a short, dark-haired man in a white button-down shirt demanded as he stepped in front of me.

I was somewhere off the main road leading to Baku, enjoying a chance to leave a stuffy Soviet-era bus for the first time in about four hours. My mouth dropped open, and I instinctively took a step back, not even sure I heard him correctly. He quietly repeated himself and pointed to a cement building a hundred feet away with signs for men's and women's toilets. I shook my head in disbelief and took another step back. Taking in the scene at this rest stop on the side of the road, I made a beeline for the only vendor selling drinks, chips and chocolate. The man followed me, repeating himself yet again. Feeling a mix of annoyance and trepidation, I turned back to face him, yelled "no," and pushed him away.

Although none of the few dozen passengers milling around the rest stop seemed to notice, the potential for causing a scene was apparently enough to dissuade the man from pursuing me any further. He lowered his head and quickly slinked away, leaving me in peace to buy a much-needed Sprite and Snickers. With my drink and chocolate bar in hand, I hurried back to the bus, breathing a sigh of relief as the door closed and we drove away.

When I emerged from the bus again three hours later in Baku, sweaty and apprehensive, a slew of taxi drivers immediately swarmed me. I pushed my way past them with several "nyets," wanting instead to find the main bus station building to check out bus schedules for later in the week. But after blowing off the cab drivers, I wandered in circles, struggling to find the entrance. Once inside, I puzzled over what appeared to be more of a shopping mall than a bus station. After finally spotting a sign for the *kassa* (cashier), I was disappointed to find that only two booths were open, neither of which could give me the information I needed. I didn't see any schedules posted anywhere. I gave up and trudged back outside into the heat and humidity of summer in Baku.

Feeling increasingly grumpy, I managed to find a bus to take me to a Metro station closer to the center of Baku. When I entered the station, I was overcome with confusion. Unlike most of the other public transit stations I found along my journey, I didn't see English anywhere in the station. They didn't even have signs with numbers and pictures showing how to buy a metro card. I stood in front of a cashier's booth for more than five minutes trying to get someone's attention to ask for help. Just as I was mumbling to myself how much I hated Baku, a man in a military uniform motioned for me to go through the turnstiles. I shook my head, saying in English that I needed to buy a card. He waved me over again, and this time another man held up a card, swiped it and motioned for me to walk through as the light turned green. I yelled out *"spasibo"* as I rushed to catch the train I could hear approaching.

Once on the crowded train, I tried to take up as little space as possible. I placed my large backpack on the floor between my legs and my smaller one on my chest. Within minutes, a young man saw I was struggling and stood up, motioning me to take his seat. Again, I smiled and breathed a sigh of relief. Maybe Baku wouldn't be so bad after all.

When I exited the metro a few stops later, I could not get my bearings. Using Google Maps before I boarded my bus to Baku, I had drawn a map to the apartment I was staying at, but as I stood on the sidewalk in the middle of an unfamiliar city, my map looked like nothing more than chicken scratches. I hesitantly approached a group of three police officers to ask for directions—hesitant because the police in the former Soviet states have a reputation for causing more problems for travelers than they solve. To my surprise, they immediately examined my map as I repeated the name of the street I needed. Soon, a crowd of about six or seven men had gathered, each offering his opinion about which way I needed to go. They soon reached a consensus, however, and sent me on my way.

Minutes later, I found myself outside the main entrance to a gated luxury apartment building in a residential area of Baku. After checking in with a security guard, I found the main lobby and took the elevator up to the third floor. There, a middle-aged woman with short hair opened the door to greet me with a smile. A member of the U.S. foreign service, Linda was the friend of a travel blogger I met on Twitter. She had been in Baku for more than a year and had an enormous apartment with a large kitchen fully stocked with American staples like Skippy peanut butter and Heinz ketchup. More importantly for me, she had an ensuite guest room with plush carpet and even plusher towels. I was uneasy about the idea of staying with yet another stranger, but Linda's offer of a free place to stay was too good to pass up. She initially only invited me to stay for two nights, but we hit it off, and she soon extended the invitation for me to stay as long as necessary to secure my onward visas to Tajikistan and Uzbekistan.

* * *

The afternoon sun glared down on me and sweat dripped from my arms as I stood in the middle of an empty street somewhere on the outskirts of Baku. I'd been wandering up and down narrow side streets off a busy road called the Badamdar Highway for more than 30 minutes, looking for the Embassy of Tajikistan. During a visit to the tourism office in Baku that morning, I was told I should take the number three bus to the municipality of Badamdar. From my own Google Maps searches of the embassy address, I knew to look for the AEF Hotel as my sign to get off the bus.

Once off the bus, though, I quickly became disoriented. None of the streets or alleyways seemed to have names or numbers that matched up with my map. I stopped at the AEF Hotel and the girl at the desk luckily spoke some English. She pointed me the way, but I missed the turn on my first try. After walking for about 10 minutes with no embassy in sight, I stopped to show the address to a man standing on the side of the dusty street.

"*Vy znayete?*" [Do you know?]

"*Nyet.*" [No.]

He opened the door to what I assumed was his home and yelled out, "Dasha!"

A woman around the same age soon appeared, with a young boy by her side. The man showed her the address, but she shook her head. At that point, I remembered I had a phone number for the Tajik embassy, which I quickly showed her. She smiled, nodded, and reached into her dress pocket to pull out her cell phone to call the embassy. Moments later, she relayed directions to the boy, who I assumed was her son. He walked me to the correct building, which turned out to be only one street over.

A small security kiosk stood outside the embassy. I waited for what felt like an eternity before being escorted inside. There, a young man greeted me in English and informed me that the consul was currently in Dushanbe, so he was handling visa requests. He directed me to a small conference room where he looked over my application and letter of invitation from the organization I'd be volunteering with in Tajikistan. Even with the LOI, I had to write a request for the visa by hand. The man dictated to me what my note should say and then told me everything should be ready the next afternoon. I asked to keep my passport and just left a copy with him, so I could take it with me to the Uzbekistan embassy. The fee would be just $35, payable when I picked up the visa.

As I was leaving the Tajik embassy, I ran into a Spanish guy who was there to pick up his visa. It turned out he had also been to the Uzbek embassy and was happy to give me directions. Go back out to the Badamdar Highway, he explained, and then walk about 500 meters. Instead of an embassy, though, I only found an old gold-toothed Azeri man who started chatting me up and telling me how much he loved Americans. I asked him if he knew where the embassy was, and he pulled me in the opposite direction from where I'd been walking. Then he flagged down a bus and asked the bus driver where the embassy was, after which he told me to get on the bus. Based on what the Spanish guy said, that didn't seem necessary, so instead I walked over to a couple men loitering outside a store and showed them the address.

Soon, a group had gathered, discussing where the embassy was and telling me I needed to take a taxi. I protested until one man called over a taxi, handed the driver a few Azeri manat and insisted I get in. Once again, I found myself in a situation where I had to strike a balance between playing it safe and trusting the kindness of strangers. I was realizing how much travel requires some level of trust or you may never get anywhere. After my experience with Berat on the way from Turkey to Tbilisi, my guard probably should have been up. But my intuition told me the men genuinely wanted to help me find the embassy. I jumped in.

Seated in the backseat of the taxi, we headed down the

Badamdar Highway back toward the center of Baku at least one kilometer, maybe two. I was soon questioning whether the driver knew where he was going. When we turned onto what could have been either a street or an alley, I was even more suspicious that I was being taken for a ride. I asked the driver in Russian again if he knew where the embassy was. He insisted he did, and sure enough, within a few minutes, he pointed to the Uzbekistan flag flying over a large mansion and a small security kiosk standing outside of the building. I thanked him profusely as I got out of the cab, feeling a bit guilty for doubting him.

As the taxi drove away, I greeted the security guard in Russian and told him I was there for a visa. Once inside the gate, I went upstairs to what looked like a doctor's office waiting room with a small cashier's window. I handed two copies of the visa application form to the man behind the glass.

"*Foto?*" he asked.

I gave him one passport-sized photo I had taken back in Chicago.

"*Pasport?*"

This time I shook my head. I needed my passport to also get my Tajik visa, so I asked him, "*Mogu li ya dat' vam kopiyu moyego pasporta?*"

"*Da, konechno,*" he replied as I handed over a photocopy of my passport.

He wrote the amount of the fee on a small slip of paper, together with the address of the bank where I needed to pay. Although the website said that processing time for U.S. citizens was two business days, he told me it would be ready the following Tuesday (four business days). After I protested, he gave me his phone number and said I could call on Monday to see if it was ready.

The next day, I managed to retrace my steps to the Tajikistan embassy without getting lost. Instead of leaving with a visa, though, the man from the previous day told me I needed to leave my passport this time and return the next afternoon. The next morning, I visited the International Bank of Azerbaijan in central Baku to pay the $160 fee for my Uzbekistan visa. The teller spoke great English and immediately asked me what country, implying multiple countries process visa payments there. I was in and out in less than five minutes. Then, it was back to the Tajikistan embassy. After a much longer wait than my previous two visits, the same young man led me into the same conference room and told me to wait. He returned about 15 minutes later with the visa stuck in my passport, the ink still drying. It was handwritten, which he clearly just did as I waited. I thanked him and walked out, relieved that I had secured at least one of my Central Asian visas.

In between the embassy visits, I fought 100-degree temperatures and 80% humidity to see as much of Baku as possible. Azerbaijan was rolling in oil money, and it was clear where they spent it. While the roads leading to the capital were often unpaved, and some of the buses seemed as old as the former Soviet Union, central Baku felt extremely modern. They rolled out the red carpet for international visitors while hosting the Eurovision song competition, and even though it had ended a week earlier, shiny new taxis emblazoned with the Eurovision logo were still prevalent.

Baku's old town was charming, still enclosed within

large stone walls. Vendors displayed colorful woven carpets for sale on the cobblestone streets, and skinny stray cats basked in the sunshine when they weren't scampering about in search of a meal. Taking the funicular up a hill above the old city, I visited Baku's extensive memorial to its fallen war heroes known as Martyr's Lane. Rows of headstones memorialized those killed in the Nagorno-Karabakh War with Armenia in the early 1990s, and an eternal flame burned below a monument overlooking the Caspian Sea. I felt uneasy, knowing how my new Armenian friends viewed the war. It occurred to me that if I had visited Azerbaijan first, I might feel completely different about the conflict that persists today.

I never figured out Baku's quirky metro system and why sometimes I needed to change trains at the May 28 station and sometimes I didn't. The ATM machines in Baku, like everywhere else in Azerbaijan, didn't seem to like my bank cards. And the high prices shocked me in comparison to neighboring Georgia and Armenia. Many items in Baku cost close to what they would in Western Europe, while others were absurdly expensive: I almost bought a pint of Baskin Robbins ice cream one scorching day before discovering it cost nearly $25.

After a weekend away in the mountain village of Lahic, I called the Uzbekistan embassy on Monday afternoon. After multiple calls and two more embassy visits, I emerged with the second of my five Central Asian visas in hand. But before I embarked on that phase of my journey, I needed to return to Yerevan.

12
Armenia (Again)

I leaned my head into the passenger side window of the taxi, rattled off an address in Russian and asked, "*Skol'ko stoit?*"

"*Dve tysyachi [2,000] dram.*"

"*Nyet,*" I said with a laugh. "*Sem'sot [700].*"

"*Dve tysyachi,*" the driver repeated, not realizing I knew very well that it should not cost that much to take a taxi to the center of Yerevan. We may have been in a parking lot on the edge of the city that doubled as a long-distance marshrutka station, but I knew no trip in Yerevan should cost more than 1,000 dram.

"*Ya znayu, chto eto ne stoit dve tysyachi,*" I shot back. "*Ya ne turist. Ya zhila zdes.*"

After scolding him that I knew better because I used to live in Yerevan, I turned to walk away in search of a more reasonable driver who wasn't trying to take advantage of an unsuspecting tourist. I had barely made it a few feet when the driver yelled back to me, "*Devushka, tysyacha [1,000], davay!*" Enjoying my minor victory, I threw my backpack into the backseat and jumped in. There was something comforting about returning to a place for the second time. Just as I felt like I knew my way around Tbilisi after multiple visits, I was grateful to arrive in Yerevan for the second time and already understand how things worked.

Fifteen minutes later, I walked into the familiar headquarters of Birthright Armenia and looked around for Angela, a fellow volunteer who had agreed to host me for a couple nights. Angela was nowhere to be found, but I saw a few other volunteers I knew and started to catch up as I kept an eye out for Angela—and Andy.

As much as I told everyone I was returning to Armenia to see more of the country, I really went back for Andy. I'd been looking forward to seeing him again ever since I walked across the border to Georgia almost two months earlier. I imagined a week of sightseeing during the day and hanging out with Andy at night, and then spending one last weekend together before I moved on to Tajikistan and the Central Asian leg of my trip.

But by the time I arrived in Yerevan, doubts began to surface. I emailed Andy with details about my arrival, and he responded with a formality that spoke volumes and made me question everything. Perhaps after traveling for eight months and meeting only one other guy I was even attracted to, I just wanted things to be more than they were. My heart was ever so slightly broken, and my ego was bruised before I'd even made it back to Yerevan. While I had planned my return with high expectations, I was mentally preparing myself to potentially be disappointed.

Angela soon appeared, and we dropped my things off at her apartment before going for dinner. I never said anything to her about Andy and me, and I had no idea if he or

Jeff had told her anything, so I resisted the urge to ask about him as we caught up over dolmas and red wine. Angela had plenty of gossip to share, but Andy's name never came up. Afterward, we headed to a popular bar called Eden to hang out with a group of volunteers who had arrived after I left. Not only was Andy not there, no one even mentioned his name. The absence of it almost seemed purposeful and sparked a feeling of paranoia. I began to suspect there was something I was missing.

The next morning, Angela and I joined more than a dozen volunteers for a day-long excursion to the Armenian countryside. I was sure Andy would be there, but as we waited for everyone to gather, there was still no sign of him. Finally, as we sat on a minibus about to depart, he appeared. My eyes followed him as he boarded the minibus, waiting for him to acknowledge my presence with at least a smile. But he walked right past me and made a beeline to sit next to another volunteer I knew from my first stint in Armenia. Sarah was a long-term volunteer around Andy's age; she'd been in Yerevan for months before I arrived. The look on her face as Andy took the seat next to her told me all I needed to know; she was clearly smitten.

Suddenly, my stomach was in knots. I searched my memory for every interaction between Andy and Sarah I could recall. Had I missed something brewing between them weeks earlier? I spent the rest of the day simultaneously avoiding them and watching them out of the corner of my eye. The looks they gave each other and the small touches they exchanged left me convinced they were seeing each other. A conversation with Angela later that night confirmed it.

I was disappointed that Andy didn't have the guts to tell me himself. He had to know I was coming back to Yerevan at least in part for him. That feeling was only made worse by wondering how many people, if any, knew about the two of us. Did Sarah know about us? It was one thing to feel like Andy rejected me; it was another to feel like it was happening somewhat publicly. And it felt even worse to feel like he rejected me for someone I not only knew but considered a sort-of friend. I had flashbacks to the unease I felt in my teens and 20s when it seemed like all my so-called friends were gossiping about my latest failed romance or unrequited crush.

I also had no idea how to handle the situation. I had no one in Yerevan to talk to about it because I'd never told anyone what happened between us. Not only was I self-conscious about our age difference, but I had been so unsure my feelings were reciprocated that I didn't even want to acknowledge them to anyone out loud.

* * *

The next day, I headed to the city of Gyumri for a couple days to see two volunteers I knew from my first stop in Armenia: Annie and Serena. I'd been eager to explore Gyumri since we had taken a day trip there back in March. The city was perhaps the oldest in Armenia and was once one of the largest in the region. A massive earthquake struck Gyumri in 1988, killing more than 50,000 people. The timing of the quake couldn't have been worse, just a few years before the collapse of the former Soviet Union and the declaration of Armenia's independence.

Following a self-guided walking tour through the center of town, I was able to learn more about the tragedy and the rebuilding. I passed numerous buildings that still lie partially in ruins, either awaiting or currently undergoing renovation—24 years after the quake. I also passed 18th and 19th century buildings made of black and red *tufa* in the historic Kumayri district of Gyumri that amazingly made it through earthquakes in both 1926 and 1988. But when I saw the occasional pile of rubble, I couldn't help but wonder if they were remnants of the earthquake as well.

Just off Gyumri's main square, I saw perhaps the most important reminder of the earthquake's damage: the St. All Saviour's Church, which was still under restoration. A small billboard in front of the church showed before and after pictures. Across the square stood the Yot Verk Cathedral, which was not as heavily damaged and was already completely restored. Several blocks from the main square stood the 19th century St. Gregory the Illuminator Church, whose dome caved in during the earthquake. I walked by a couple times without even realizing a church once stood there—as a neighborhood church that served the working-class population, renovation efforts had not even started.

That night, as Annie, Serena and I headed outside of Gyumri to watch the sunset, Annie pointed out shacks that were originally intended as temporary housing after the earthquake but that were still occupied in recent years. And on the outskirts of the city stood multiple apartment buildings, begun in the years following the earthquake but never completed when Armenia's economy struggled in the post-Soviet years.

My two days in Gyumri were just what I needed: a chance to experience more of Armenia on my own without the cloud of Andy and Sarah's relationship hanging over my head and the opportunity to get to know Annie and Serena better, building friendships that would last well beyond my trip. But as I rode back to Yerevan, my thoughts returned to Andy. Never one for confrontation or difficult conversations, I couldn't see myself directly asking him about Sarah. I felt the best I could hope for was for him to bring it up himself, but I knew the chances of that were remote.

* * *

I stumbled along the empty streets of Yerevan, singing to myself as I tried to make my way back to my hostel around 3 a.m.

First, it was Adele and the song Andy and I danced to weeks before. Then it was Cee Lo and lyrics that had nothing to do with my current situation aside from the "fuck you" in the chorus. While I never had any musical talent whatsoever, I often turned to song lyrics to help me process my emotions and express my feelings, especially when it came to failed romances. It often amazed me how singers I'd never met seemed to be able to tap into my state of mind and find the words to perfectly describe how I felt in any given situation.

After a long night out drinking with a group of volunteers, I'd flipped the switch from sadness over Andy to anger and spite. I wanted to have the best week of my entire trip, not just for myself but also to show Andy that I didn't care. I didn't want him to see how much I was hurting, but at the same time, I recognized he probably wasn't even paying attention. I also knew from experience that, for me, the best way to get over someone was to stay as busy as possible. After my relationship with Patrick ended, I threw myself into marathon training, volleyball leagues, and Chicago street fairs, determined not to spend a single weekend night at home. Despite being an introvert and finding too much social interaction exhausting, I wanted to surround myself with friends who would build me back up again. I didn't want to give myself any opportunity to dwell on how awful I felt.

The same was true after I realized Andy was with Sarah. After returning from Gyumri, I spent my days on organized tours outside of Yerevan. One cloudy day I visited Geghard Monastery and Garni Temple, both in magnificent settings not far from Yerevan. Garni was an impressive Greek temple standing on the edge of a cliff while Geghard stood in a steep canyon. Geghard was home to more than a dozen cave churches and allegedly once held the holy lance that pierced Christ's side at the crucifixion. Another day, my tour included the picturesque Noravank Monastery, which featured the only two-story church I could recall seeing in Armenia or elsewhere. To reach the second level, visitors had to crawl up a precarious narrow stone staircase on the outside of the building.

After my daytime sightseeing, I spent my evenings enjoying Yerevan's vibrant outdoor café and bar scene. I spent every night watching EuroCup games with Alex, a cute volunteer I had barely talked to the first time around. It may have been the most at home I felt during my entire trip. I felt like I was back in Chicago, meeting up with friends to watch the NBA or Stanley Cup playoffs. Not having to volunteer in the morning or return to my homestay by the midnight curfew meant I could just chill and have fun, staying out until 2 a.m. or 4 a.m. or even later if I wanted to.

I only saw Andy once more. I never did get the nerve to try to talk to him about Sarah. Our goodbye came in front of a dozen people at a crowded bar. As he hugged me goodbye, he half-heartedly told me to let him know if I ever came through his hometown of Los Angeles. That was as close as I would come to closure.

* * *

I jolted up in bed as the alarm on my Blackberry went off. It was lying next to me in my hostel bed rather than on the nightstand, a result of how drunk I was when I fell into bed just a few hours earlier.

My last night in Yerevan started with Mexican food and margaritas at Cactus with Lillian and Alex. We soon met up with Angela and others to go bar hopping from Bourbon Street to Calumet to That Place. I downed vodka shots and danced until my feet hurt—and found myself flirting with Greg, a cute volunteer I'd met earlier in the week.

By the time we got to That Place, an underground bar in central Yerevan that didn't get busy until most other bars had closed, we were arm-in-arm, and it wasn't long before we were kissing. I had been so self-conscious about kissing Andy in public, but with Greg, I didn't even care. I almost wanted people to see us so that word would get back to Andy. Deep down, I knew he wouldn't care, but it made me feel better in the moment. We closed the bar down, and he walked me back to my hostel as the sun came up. I had no idea how I even thought to set my alarm to wake up for my marshrutka back to Tbilisi the next morning.

I ignored the pounding in my head and sprang out of bed. It was 9:30 a.m. I quickly threw on a new tank top, clean underwear and jeans, washed my face and brushed my teeth. I stuffed everything I could into my bags before throwing my hair into a ponytail and running downstairs to hail a taxi to take me to the same marshrutka station I'd arrived at eight days earlier. Within 30 minutes, I was sitting in the backseat of a marshrutka, returning to Tbilisi for the last time.

Serena happened to be in Tbilisi on a visa run so we met up for dinner the next night. After a couple glasses of Georgian wine, I confessed everything to her about me and Andy. I was relieved when she expressed surprise—she hadn't heard anything—and encouraged when she conveyed her befuddlement about Andy and Sarah getting together. By the end of the evening, I felt like Serena and I had solidified a friendship that would continue once we both returned home. I realized that, while my return trip to Armenia didn't turn out as planned, it was still worthwhile. Not only did I see more of the country on my own, I developed deeper friendships with the other volunteers.

Soon, I would put all thoughts of Andy behind me as I hopped on a plane to start the final part of my year-long adventure: Central Asia and the former Soviet states often referred to as "the 'Stans."

PART THREE
June-September

PART 3: JUNE-SEPTEMBER

13
Tajikistan

"*Privet. Menya zovut Katya. U menya yest' bron'*," I said to a young woman behind a small glass window in the lobby of a dreary hotel in Dushanbe, the capital of Tajikistan.

"*Mne zhal'. U menya net bronirovaniya na vas*," she replied apologetically.

She didn't have a reservation for me.

"*I u nas net nomerov*," she added.

Even worse, the hotel had no rooms.

My empty stomach growled, and I could feel a tear begin to well up in my eye.

"*No, u menya yest' bron'*," I insisted as she handed me the reservation list—handwritten in pencil on an eight-by-five piece of paper. I had a reservation.

I frowned with dismay as I scanned the paper for my name and realized that it was not there. It was 7 a.m. and all I wanted to do was crawl into bed and fall asleep. Instead, it seemed I'd be headed out to the tree-lined streets of Dushanbe to try to find a hotel with an available room. Considering how difficult it had been to book a hotel room in the first place, I was not optimistic about my chances.

After two flight delays, I'd landed in Dushanbe before dawn. I spent the next two hours waiting in line to go through immigration—two booths for foreigners staffed by the slowest-typing border guards I had encountered on my entire trip. Once I was through, I nervously headed to the next room to find my backpack—a fellow passenger on my flight from Istanbul told me the flight crew informed him his bag didn't make it. I breathed a sigh of relief to see that mine was one of three still sitting on the floor.

As I exited the airport, I kept my eyes peeled for an ATM or currency exchange but saw none. Eventually, I asked one of the many taxi drivers swarming around. Since he wanted to get paid, he led me to a currency exchange where I changed just $20 to prevent him from seeing how much money I had and trying to overcharge me (which he did anyway). A short ride later and I was walking into the dark, empty lobby of the Hotel Vakhsh. It was not my first choice of a place to stay in Dushanbe, but it was the only place affordable and available—or so I thought.

Facing the prospect of the Hotel Vakhsh not having a room for me, all the emotions that had been simmering for the past few weeks finally bubbled to the surface—the stress, the disappointment, the sadness, the fear, the anxiety. It all hit me at once, and the tears started to surge uncontrollably as I collapsed onto an old couch in the hotel lobby. The prior three months had been the best of my trip. I caught up with old friends and forged new relationships. I had more fun in the weeks I spent in Armenia, Italy, and Turkey than the rest of my trip combined. I found a comfort zone in Georgia and Armenia that made it hard to leave. But I was physically exhausted from a hectic last week in Yerevan, and I was mentally exhausted from the stress of getting my visas, the disappointment of things not progressing with Andy the way I'd hoped, and the sadness of saying goodbye to people who became good friends. And, perhaps more than anything, I was terrified of what was coming next.

As I sat on the sagging floral sofa in the lobby of the Hotel Vakhsh, a woman rambled something to me in Russian that I didn't understand. I gave her a blank stare and just kept crying until another woman appeared. They carefully explained to me that there was one free room. I could look at it and, if I liked it, it was mine. They led me up a massive stone staircase to the second floor and ushered me into a decent size room with décor that hadn't been updated since Soviet times. A tiny twin bed covered by a thin floral print bedspread sat in one corner, and a 1980s television set was perched on a wooden table across the room. A rotating fan stood at the foot of the bed. The bathroom was missing one key component: a sink. But I tried the water in the shower, and it came out clear and hot, so I nodded and said, "*Khorosho*."

As soon as the women left, I turned the fan on high and pointed it straight onto the bed. I collapsed on top of the scratchy comforter and closed my eyes, relieved to have a place to sleep. My mind was still racing, and soon, tears were flowing again. In 10 months on the road to that point, I'd survived miserable homestays, freezing temperatures, long ferry rides, and Turkish scam artists. I crossed over a dozen land borders without major incident, even making it into Azerbaijan, where many people said I would hit a roadblock. I had so much to be proud of. Yet the 'Stans—Tajikistan, Uzbekistan, Turkmenistan, Kazakhstan, and Kyrgyzstan—just felt like they would be more difficult. The tourism infrastructure in Central Asia was almost non-existent, and I could find little practical information online. With my blonde hair and blue eyes, I feared I would stand out more than I had yet, at least since Ulan Ude. I also had no idea how effective my Russian language skills would be in countries where Russian may not be the lingua franca. And I knew it would be hot, with temperatures soaring above 100 degrees Fahrenheit, much hotter than I was used to.

I wanted to believe that I had grown throughout my travels, that I was more confident and comfortable with myself than ever before. I wanted to believe that I could handle whatever the 'Stans would throw at me. Despite it all, I was terrified. And so when I fell onto the rock-hard twin bed in the worst hotel I'd seen in 10 months, I just kept crying until I finally managed to fall asleep.

* * *

Five hours later, I woke up to the midday sun heating my room like an oven and my stomach rumbling. With no sink, I washed my face using the faucet in the shower and headed out to withdraw cash, buy a SIM card, and find food. I was relieved when just a few blocks away, I found an ATM that would take my debit card. I happily withdrew enough Tajik somoni to last me a month and then withdrew US dollars with my other card to add to my backup stash for later travel in the 'Stans. Next, I headed to the Tcell store to get a SIM card. This should have been easy enough, but the clerk insisted on seeing my registration form. This was a holdover from Soviet times when officials required all visitors to the Soviet Union to register with local authorities to track their movement through the country. By the time I started my journey, only Russia and several Central Asian states clung to this intrusive tradition. Indeed, Tajikistan had recently abolished the rule for people visiting on tourist visas and staying less than 30 days as I was. But the clerk behind the counter didn't seem to know about this change.

I left to look for another option and only had to go a couple blocks before I saw a Beeline store. This was one of the benefits of all my months of travel through the former Soviet states: I recognized Beeline as a common cell phone provider I had used in Russia and Georgia. There, they were not only willing to sell me a SIM card without a registration form, but the girl behind the counter spoke English, making the entire transaction seamless. My final stop was a familiar one—a Southern Fried Chicken fast-food restaurant. I discovered this chain in Yerevan and assumed it was Armenian (I later learned it was a British chain), so I was shocked and thrilled to find one in Dushanbe—something familiar was exactly what I needed. My lunch of chicken shashlik, French fries, and coleslaw totally hit the spot.

By this point, the heat was starting to take its toll on me, but since I only had a single day to explore Dushanbe, I wasn't ready to succumb to the heat quite yet. Luckily, Rudaki Avenue—a wide, tree-lined street that was Dushanbe's main drag—provided some much-needed shade. It didn't feel all that different from boulevards in other former Soviet capitals, with a mix of decently manicured parks, imposing government buildings and audacious monuments to former leaders or cult heroes. I was right at home.

As I reluctantly walked back to the Hotel Vakhsh for a much-needed full night of sleep, I watched the sky turn deep shades of blue, orange, and purple as the sun set over Dushanbe. I suddenly wished I could stay another day. I wanted to see more of what this capital had to offer, and I was starting to think perhaps the 'Stans may not be so bad.

* * *

"*Tebe luchshe govorit' po-russki*," the bearded man said to me with a slight smile. We had just been introduced, and he was already telling me I should speak Russian better.

Sarvar was probably around my parents' age, but years of tending to sheep and cattle in the sun and wind in the Fann Mountains left his brown skin wrinkled and dry. He looked like he could've been my grandfather. His wife, Mouhayo, sat to his left. She shook her head and looked down, clearly used to his criticisms. Despite the afternoon heat, she wore a long-sleeved floral dress paired with a matching head scarf that was tied in a knot behind her head. This seemed to be the Tajik style. While the country was predominantly Muslim, the women I saw in Dushanbe didn't wear hijabs that covered their ears and neck as I'd seen in other majority Muslim countries. Rather, their fashionable head scarves not only exposed their ears and neck but sometimes showed an inch or two of their hairlines as well.

We sat outside on a free-standing porch-like structure called a *tapchan*. Common throughout Tajikistan and Uzbekistan, it was covered with colorful mattresses called *kurpachas* and featured a low table in the middle where Mouhayo had meticulously poured four cups of tea. Next to me sat Stefania, a tall Italian woman who was the volunteer coordinator for the Zerafshan Tourism Development Association. The ZTDA was a community-based tourism organization in Tajikistan's Fann Mountains and Zerafshan Valley in the northwestern part of the country. It offered homestays and guided activities like hiking and horseback riding. But I wasn't sitting with Sarvar and Mouhayo as a tourist; I was there to teach them English.

Sarvar's critique of my Russian skills stung. While I knew I wasn't fluent, I thought I'd improved dramatically during my time traveling in Ukraine, Moldova, Georgia and Azerbaijan, speaking almost nothing but Russian. Indeed, I beamed with pride when I arrived in Chisinau, Moldova, and the man at the currency exchange assumed I was Russian. I evaded a potential scammer using Russian on my way from Turkey to Tbilisi. And I navigated my way around Baku to obtain two Central Asian visas. But my nerves got the best of me as I met my hosts; I fumbled with simple phrases, and I struggled to understand Sarvar's Tajik accent. As we wrapped up introductions and Stefania got in her Jeep to return to Penjikent, more than 40 kilometers away, I worried that I was in over my head.

As soon as Stefania's Jeep was out of sight, Mouhayo gestured at me to follow her into the house. My bedroom for the next two weeks was connected to the rest of the house but had a separate entrance. It was large enough to sleep a dozen or more tourists. Stacks of *kurpachas* and thick duvets lined the room, and a low table sat on one end, like the one on the *tapchan* outside. I gave a nod of approval to Mouhayo and dropped my things before we continued the tour. The toilet and shower were in a separate building across a small yard, and a small sink and mirror were set up outside a few feet from the outhouse. I soon learned that the pipes were all connected, so when I wanted to shower, the water to the sink had to be turned off. To get a hot shower, the water heater had to be turned on for at least 15 minutes. I immediately decided I would limit my showers to every other day, something I was quite used to by this point.

* * *

I stared at my computer screen, anxiously waiting for my Yahoo email account to load. While there was no Wi-Fi in the Fann Mountains, Stefania had left me with a 3G wireless internet stick. It plugged into my laptop like a USB drive and was supposed to give me internet access for the next month. So far, it had failed to connect. I was about to give up when I heard a knock on my door. I opened it to see a young girl in a short-sleeved paisley dress and purple vest staring up at me. Her thick hair was tied back with a mustard yellow head scarf, and behind her stood another seemingly younger girl. The second girl wore no scarf but instead had her jet-black hair plaited in a braid that fell to the middle of her back. She broke out in giggles as soon as I said hello.

Sarvar had sent his youngest daughter Mohpisand, just 14 years old, and her cousin Farhunda, 12 years old, to take me on a walk around the village. The village was called Shing, which appropriately meant "green pasture" in the ancient Sogdian language, which had roots in Persian and was a predecessor to the modern Tajik language. Around 1,700 people lived in Shing then, but many had left over the years after a series of earthquakes and mudslides wrought havoc on the village. Only men in Shing worked outside the home, most as farmers, cattle herders, or craftsmen. The village had a school, a hospital, and two mosques. I read somewhere that about 200 villagers had completed higher education, which seemed high for a mountain village in Tajikistan.

Mohpisand and Farhunda whispered to each other in Tajik as they led me along dirt roads past homes made of concrete bricks until we reached a mosque that wasn't much larger than many of the houses. I was at a complete loss for what to say until finally, I thought to ask if they spoke Russian. Mohpisand responded affirmatively, so I asked a few questions to try to break the ice:

"*Skol'ko tebe let?*" [How old are you?]

"*Skol'ko u tebya brat'yev i sester?*" [How many brothers and sisters do you have?]

"*Kak ikh zovut?*" [What are their names?]

Mophisand answered each question in such a whisper, I strained to hear her. Farhunda quickly jumped in, repeating what her cousin said. They seemed too shy to ask me any questions, but their faces lit up when I took my camera out of my bag. For the next 10 minutes, they took turns posing outside of the mosque, eagerly checking the viewfinder of the camera after each shot. All the initial awkwardness faded away. I was excited to see what would come next.

* * *

The next morning, I emerged from my room after breakfast to see Mohpisand, Farhunda, Mouhayo, and close to a dozen family members gathered on the *tapchan* outside. Before arriving in Shing, I understood I would be teaching English to Sarvar and his eldest son, who together ran their homestay and guiding business. The sight of his daughters and multiple grandchildren, ranging from 10-year-old Mehron to 30-something mothers Mavzuna and Ganjina, came as a shock. I tried not to panic—or at least to not let them see that I was panicking. I started with a lesson that would teach me as much as it might teach them: asking and answering the question, "What is your name?" By the time two hours had passed, though, I had used most of the material I had prepared for my first few days of lessons. I was in trouble.

After our afternoon lesson, Ganjina's oldest daughter, 16-year-old Jonona, took me for a walk. As we strolled along the gravel road leading to the center of the village, she blurted out that she loved me. I stopped in my tracks, at a loss for how to react. Love is not a word I throw around lightly. Indeed, it isn't a word I even grew up hearing or saying a lot. Even prior to my parents' divorce, I have no memory of them being affectionate or saying, "I love you," and I don't recall them saying it often to my brother or me. The same was true of my grandparents on both sides of my family. And when it came to romantic relationships, while there had been a couple men who I thought I loved at the time, I never got to the point where I said the word. For a teenager who just met me to say it so freely threw me far outside of my comfort zone. I had no idea how to respond.

To say it back felt disingenuous, but to ignore it seemed even worse. I awkwardly smiled back at Jonona, nodded and kept walking.

As uncomfortable as I was, Jonona's declaration reinforced for me how excited the entire family was for me to be there. Mouhayo meant it when she said that I would be another daughter to her. Indeed, on the same walk, Jonona asked me if I had any sisters, and when I said no, she said she would be my sister. The next evening, Shohpisand visited me in my room, bearing an English phrase book that she used to try to converse with me. Before she left, she gave me a big hug and declared she loved me as well.

* * *

I sat in my room, flustered and close to tears. After using up all my planned lessons the first morning, I had no clue how I was going to come up with four hours of English lessons every day for two weeks. I thought I had prepared myself for this situation. I took an online course in Teaching English as a Foreign Language (TEFL) before leaving home, and I trusted it taught me a lot. In retrospect, the one thing it didn't cover was how to teach total beginners. When it came to lesson planning, I was able to select the level for which I planned my lessons, and I always chose intermediate. At that time, I never pictured myself working with beginners or with children. I expected to be teaching adults in Tajikistan, not Sarvar's extended family. Everyone was at a beginner level, but they caught on at different rates, so it was hard to balance teaching what many still needed to practice while not completely boring the others.

A picture dictionary that I picked up on a whim in Tbilisi saved me. I used it to teach the alphabet and pronunciation, as well as numbers, days, months, colors, action words, food, and clothing. While I initially started or ended lessons by simply saying and repeating words or asking everyone to take turns reading the words, I eventually branched out. Once I taught action words, I pointed to animals in the dictionary and asked them to say what each animal does. When we learned colors, I did the same, asking what color different animals and objects were.

I eventually settled into a rhythm with two hours of lessons in the morning and two hours of lessons in the afternoon. I used the morning lessons to review and expand on what we learned the previous day, and I introduced new concepts in the afternoon. Each lesson began with a short review, but I soon realized that the more I taught, the more there was to review. I could use that to fill some time. I also observed that everyone dutifully took notes on just about every word that came out of my mouth—to the point where I realized that if I gave them a lot of new vocabulary to write, it took up more time. That may not have been the recommended approach, but they seemed to benefit from the repetition and the writing.

I also tried to mix things up by playing games. After we learned action words, I introduced charades, acting out the words they learned. It took them a while to get the hang of it; many would announce their action before doing it instead of waiting for people to guess. But it worked, and they seemed to be both learning and having fun. When we moved on to 20 Questions, the kids loved sticking pieces of paper to their foreheads with the names of animals that they were trying to guess. My most exciting breakthrough may have been teaching them how to pronounce the sound "th." I discovered that in the phrasebooks they had, the "th" sound is translated as either "c" or "z" because there is no equivalent sound in Russian or Tajik. I noticed how much they struggled with the sound as we worked through the dictionary, so I spent a few minutes demonstrating where they needed to put their tongue to make the "th." In addition to drawing a lot of laughs, I think most of them got it.

The more time I spent with the family, the more they put me at ease. Mouhayo, Ganjina, and Shohpisand regularly lamented the fact that I couldn't eat the overflowing plates of plov and tomato and cucumber salad they put in front of me. I tried in vain to explain I was simply full—there was too much food! Mouhayo also got a kick out of my terrified look when she spoke of killing chickens, making a throat-slashing motion as she said the word "chicken." And the whole family couldn't stop laughing as I tried to ride a donkey in the mountains. Mohpisand became my personal guide, taking me on walks around the village and leading me hiking up into the mountains on Sundays with Farhunda or one of her other cousins in tow. When Mohpisand wasn't available, Jonona or Shohpisand enthusiastically took her place. And when I returned from one hike in the middle of a thunderstorm, Mouhayo had a hot meal waiting for me and insisted I immediately take a hot shower while she washed my muddy clothes.

While the prospect of daily English lessons continued to make me anxious, they were often full of smiles—and laughs. The kids were their own harshest critics, often chiding each other when someone accidentally answered in Russian or Tajik instead of English. Mohpisand got the giggles as she asked Farhunda if she had a donkey (she didn't), and 11-year-old Boborjan drew laughs as he asked 14-year-old Dodojan if he had a woman (he apparently did). And everyone cracked up when six-year-old Mehron grabbed my sticky note with the word "baby" written on it and proudly stuck it on his chest.

My two weeks in Shing flew by. As much as Dodojan rolled his eyes at me and urged me to keep going while I waited for the others to grasp something, Mohpisand, Mehron, and Farhunda seemed to hang on every word I said. It was gratifying to me that by the time I went for a walk with Jonona and Shohpisand a few nights before I left, they were using bits of English and asking me what things were called as we walked. The next day, when Mohpisand, Farhunda, and Boborjan took me hiking, Mohpisand tried to use English whenever she could and constantly inquired about what things were called—a shortcut, a shadow, a rock, steep, flat. And while Boborjan wasn't quite as curious, he did use the word "jump" at every opportunity. In the end, I felt like I made a difference.

Mouhayo, Ganjina, and the others told me they would cry when I left. If I didn't like my second homestay, I could return to Shing. Shohpisand even came to my room and begged me not to leave. They invited me to come back to Shing the following summer with my parents, and Sarvar spoke of trying to speak by Skype when I returned to the United States. In an incredibly warm-hearted gesture, they decided I needed a traditional Tajik dress and pants as a parting gift. Mouhayo joked that when people would see me in it, they would think I was not American but a Tajik girl. Their excitement as they measured me for the outfit and then sat on the floor, carefully sewing it together, was contagious.

On the morning of my departure, Mouhayo, Ganjina, Jonona, Mouhayo's daughter-in-law Husniya, Farhunda, and Mohpisand took turns embracing me and giving me three kisses, alternating cheeks. Then Mohpisand grabbed the smaller of my two backpacks and dutifully swung it onto her back to carry it out to the Jeep waiting to take me to my next homestay in the village of Padrud. The rest of the family followed. As I settled into the front seat of the Jeep, they all stood less than a foot away, waving goodbye and wiping away a few stray tears as I did the same. It was by far the most difficult farewell of my entire trip.

14

Uzbekistan

As my hotel room in Khujand filled with light, I checked my Blackberry to see it was just after 5 a.m. I lay awake thinking about what the day had in store. It was my last morning in Tajikistan, and the day I would move on to Uzbekistan. After leaving Sarvar and Mouhayo, I spent two weeks in another mountain village with a family that was not nearly as welcoming. I breathed a sigh of relief when Stefania's Jeep appeared to take me back to Penjikent. The ride from Penjikent to Khujand had been gorgeous and precarious, crossing high mountain passes while squeezed into a shared taxi with three others. I only had one afternoon to explore Khujand as my visa would expire the next day.

I was dreading the border crossing. Uzbekistan and Tajikistan didn't have the best relationship, and I'd heard that Uzbek officials could be difficult. I also had no clue how I would get to the border. Although Lonely Planet said a taxi from Khujand should be $15, drivers I asked the previous day quoted me 200 Tajik somoni—the equivalent of $40. I didn't want to pay that much—and didn't have that much somoni left.

I decided instead to try to take a marshrutka to a town called Buston, from where I could get a much cheaper shared taxi. However, after waiting 20 minutes in the scorching morning sun with no marshrutka in sight, I tried one last time to hail a taxi. Once again, the driver quoted me 200 somoni to the border. But this time, when I declined, he offered to take me to a bus station on the edge of town for 25 somoni. He said there I could catch a shared taxi the rest of the way. Luckily, he was correct.

By 8:30, I was sitting in the backseat of a taxi with a friendly Tajik woman—for a fare of just 60 somoni. The ride was much longer than I expected, but the time passed quickly as my seatmate and I chatted in Russian. She was on her way to see her parents in Uzbekistan for the first time in a year. The family was separated when the Soviet Union disintegrated, and now they required visas to visit each other—something they could do only once a year for 10 days at a time. By the time we reached the border, she had shown me pictures of her kids and taken a picture of us together on her cell phone. I hoped my new friend might help guide me through the immigration process entering Uzbekistan, but she was held back as we departed Tajikistan.

Leaving Tajikistan took just minutes as the immigration officer barely glanced at my passport before stamping it and waving me through. But as I approached the immigration and customs building on the Uzbekistan side, my heart sank. Dozens of people were lined up in front of a window with just one officer. Around the edges of the small room, people hovered over customs forms, carefully filling in the blanks. After completing two copies of the form, I entered the fray, trying to secure a place in one of multiple lines. While I read on a travel blog about friendly Tajiks knowing how to queue so well, I was surrounded by Tajik women who seemed to think it was their mission to make sure I never made it to the front. After an hour of getting bumped to the side by pushy women waiting to shove their passports over to the single officer on duty, I had enough.

As I finally neared the front of the line, I saw another woman slide her passport past mine and I snapped. I declared loudly, "*Ya byla zdes' pervoi.*" I was here first.

I don't know if the officer behind the window heard me or if he just finally noticed the tallest, blondest woman in the room, but he pushed the Tajik passport aside.

"*Dayte mne vash pasport,*" he said, looking directly at me. I smiled and handed him my passport. Within minutes, he stamped me into Uzbekistan and led me past the throng of people to the other side of a metal barrier.

While I was grateful to be through immigration, I still had to clear customs. I stood nervously as I waited for a scowling officer to review my forms. I watched as he made marks here and there, eventually circling the section where I declared how much cash I was carrying. Uzbek officials were known to be notoriously strict about how much money people bring in and out of the country. I was told to carefully declare all the cash that I had. Knowing that working ATMs would be hard to find in Uzbekistan, I stocked up on US dollars in advance and came in carrying over $1,400 and 80,000 Uzbek soms—about $40 worth that I changed at the border. I didn't think twice about such an amount, but as I stood waiting to go through customs, I saw a sign that seemed to indicate that you couldn't bring in more than $1,000, so I was doubly nervous. I had also heard that prickly guards might decide to search my belongings or ask me invasive questions, but luckily no one was feeling difficult. They let me through without any hassle. By 11 a.m., I had settled into the back of a taxi with a cold bottle of water for the 90-minute ride to Tashkent, the capital of Uzbekistan.

* * *

I was nearly giddy as my taxi pulled up in front of the Hotel Uzbekistan in Tashkent. After a month of homestays and shabby hotels in Tajikistan, I was staring at a real hotel again. I walked into a bright, shiny lobby and was hit by a blast of cold air—my first taste of air conditioning since I'd been in Georgia. I soon learned the hotel had all the modern conveniences I no longer took for granted: a concierge, 24-hour café, a souvenir shop, electronic key cards, free Wi-Fi and cotton-soft toilet paper.

As I ventured out later that day to explore Tashkent, I couldn't help but compare it to Dushanbe. Tashkent felt much larger, with multiple vast boulevards and large landscaped parks. Sparkling new buildings stood throughout the city center. Tashkent also had a plethora of supermarkets and stoplights, a subway system and Western clothing stores like Benetton and Mango. While most Tajik women seemed to wear ankle-length dresses and covered their hair with scarves, women in Tashkent dressed in more Western attire—tank tops, short skirts, shorts and high heels were common. I saw more foreigners in Tashkent and I didn't receive nearly the number of comments or stares that I did in Dushanbe. Indeed, I felt like I blended in surprisingly well. It occurred to me later that people probably assumed I was Russian.

As I walked around Tashkent, the sun beating down on me and temperatures soaring far above 100, several other things caught my eye. For a city of nearly two million people, it was incredibly quiet. I chalked it up to the heat and assumed everyone must come out at night when it cooled down, but the first evening I went out to dinner, returning after dark, the sidewalks remained empty. I was surprised at the noticeable police presence—more so than any place I had visited since Moscow. Officers seemed to stand at every corner, at the entrance to every subway station and in front of just about any important-looking building. To my relief, I interacted with the police only once during my stay, and it was to ask for directions. Others I met were not so lucky. A Belgian couple looked at me in shock when I told them I had been walking around without my passport while waiting for my Kazakhstan visa; they had been stopped and asked for theirs every single time they rode the subway.

Just as I spent 10 days in Vilnius waiting for my visa to Belarus, I stayed in Tashkent for 10 days as I tried to secure a visa to Kazakhstan. It proved to be a much-needed break and mental reset. After living with families for much of the previous few months, I savored being alone again. I spent hours lounging in my air-conditioned room watching BBC World News and surfing the internet. The scorching heat deterred me from spending too much time sightseeing; the four trips I had to make to the Kazakhstan embassy provided enough time in the hot July sun. It was also a reminder that I didn't need to spend every minute of my trip discovering something new or immersing myself in the local culture. When traveling long-term, it's almost impossible to maintain that kind of pace. Taking time to relax and do nothing was valuable as well.

* * *

As I wandered through the center of old Bukhara, I suddenly stopped and did a double take. A small white car was parked in front of me, covered in decals. As drivers surrounded me, pushing their taxi services, I stepped closer to the car to confirm that it was what I thought it was: a Mongol Rally car. The Mongol Rally was a road race for charity. Each year, teams drove from London to Mongolia over several weeks in the middle of the summer, often squeezing into vehicles that weren't really meant to be driven nearly 6,000 miles in a single trip. I first heard of the rally the previous summer when my friend and travel blogger Sherry teamed up with two other bloggers for the adventure. It particularly intrigued me because teams must cross one or more of Ukraine, Russia, Kazakhstan, Uzbekistan, and/or Turkmenistan to get to Mongolia—all countries on my itinerary. This summer, I knew of two other bloggers who joined forces for the rally, and since the timing coincided with my travels through the region, I'd been following along.

Despite that, it never occurred to me that I might personally encounter any rally teams in Bukhara. Feeling energized by the prospect of meeting a team (and fellow tourists to possibly hang out with), I debated what to do next.

The car was parked in front of a small hotel, so I went inside and inquired at the front desk.

"*Ty znayesh', komu prinadlezhit belaya mashina?*" [Do you know who owns the white car?]

"*Da, oni zdes' gosti. Troye muzhchin.*" [Yes. They're guests here. Three men.]

"*Oni zdes' seychas?*" [Are they here now?]

"*Nyet.*" [No.]

From this exchange, I learned that the owners of the car—three men—were staying there, but they weren't currently around. So I left a note with my email address and the name of my hotel. What did I have to lose?

This kind of gesture was nothing new for me. Back in high school, I developed a crush on a guy staying at the same Keystone, Colorado ski resort as my family on spring break. After returning home, I wrote to the manager of the small resort asking for the guy's address and the manager obliged. Even more surprising, my crush actually wrote back to me and sent his class photo, although it would be the only time I would hear from him. Years later, I was delivering newspapers in college when I realized that a guy I liked was on my route. I did what any rom-com heroine would do and left a note with his newspaper one day, leaving my phone number and telling him to call me. That didn't pan out, but at least I never had to wonder, "What if?" Indeed, in each case, I had no expectations. If anything came of my efforts, I would be pleasantly surprised. At the same time, I avoided the potential embarrassment of a face-to-face rejection.

Hours later, as I was in my hotel room getting ready

for bed, I nearly jumped when my phone rang—it was the receptionist downstairs telling me, "Three men here to see you." It took me a few seconds to connect the dots, but I quickly realized it was the guys from the Mongol Rally and hurried down to the lobby. There, I found three dark-haired Brits who introduced themselves as Adam, Adrian, and Antonio. I soon learned that their team's name was "The Wrong Way Around"—a take-off on Ewan McGregor's series, *Long Way Round*, which also happened to be an inspiration for my trip. Hitting it off easily, we soon moved to the hotel courtyard to chat more over drinks. Three hours and a couple bottles of wine later, they returned to their hotel, and I went to bed with an invitation to join them the next morning for a tour of Bukhara led by the son of the owner of their hotel.

As I went to meet them at 9:30 the next morning, it occurred to me that I might be imposing—it was only Adam who had invited me. I momentarily considered backing out, but as soon as we all met up, I realized I was overthinking things. Whenever I felt like I was imposing before, I probably wasn't, and I may have missed out on opportunities to form connections as a result. This time, I decided to go with the flow and enjoy myself. For the next four hours, 15-year-old Akhmad showed us around Bukhara. A center of trade, culture and religion along the ancient Silk Road, the city was home to more than a hundred architectural monuments and the old city center was a UNESCO World Heritage Site. The old city felt ancient, dusty, and overflowing with history. We started with the Lyab-i Hauz, a large rectangular pond surrounded by mulberry trees, tea houses and blue-tiled madrassahs. From there, we strolled through covered bazaars and visited the 12th century Kalon Mosque and its towering minaret, once the tallest building in Central Asia. While it was closed to visitors, we stopped outside the massive Ark fortress. With walls 60 feet tall, the huge military structure dated back to the fifth century. Coming from a country with mere hundreds of years of history, it was hard for me to even fathom a building that had stood for more than a millennium.

The guys haggled over silly Soviet-era hats at an outdoor market, and then we hopped into the Mongol Rally car to head out of town to the Emir's Summer Palace. While the palace's expansive grounds and colorful interiors gave us a sense of how Bukharan royalty lived in the early 19th century, the real highlight might have been a funky, multi-sided Russian mirror. We took turns standing in the mirror while taking selfies before selfies were really a thing. By early afternoon, it was time for the guys to move on to Samarkand—they had already stayed in Bukhara longer than any other stop on their journey. We exchanged email addresses and said goodbye, promising to keep in touch. I returned to my hotel, happy that my small risk in leaving a note for them had paid off.

* * *

After lunch, I was ready to see more of Bukhara on my own. I hadn't gone far when I discovered a 16th century madrassah that appeared to be open. An elderly caretaker immediately greeted me as I stepped inside. He took me by the arm and drew my attention to the detailed designs on the ceiling before explaining the history of the madrassah in Russian. The caretaker led me into a side room with a complete model of Bukhara and showed me the location of just about every mosque and madrassah in the city. Then, he encouraged me to explore and pointed out that I could climb up to the second floor of the building. Most of the sites I visited in Uzbekistan were regulated with ticket sales and guards and signs and ropes blocking off the places you just couldn't go. The fact that this caretaker was pushing me to scramble all over this ancient madrassah was an amazing surprise. It reminded me of my clamber up the minaret in Ani with the security guard Orhan.

A group of French tourists entered the madrassah just before me, so naturally I did my best to avoid them. I watched as they ascended the narrow stone staircase to the second floor, and as soon as they descended again, I took my chance. After snapping a few pictures of the courtyard from the balcony, I noticed another set of stairs leading upwards. With no signs prohibiting the climb, I carefully ascended, coming out on the roof. Knowing that the madrassah was around 400 years old, I tiptoed from the top step onto the roof, half expecting it to collapse below me.

While the roof offered a nice look down into the courtyard of the madrassah, my view of the rest of the city wasn't too impressive. I was too nervous to stray far from the stairs, unsure if I should even be up there in the first place. After less than five minutes, I carefully made my way back down. When I returned to the second floor, I realized that multiple corridors led away from the balconies facing the courtyard, giving me access to nearly the entire second level. I took my time exploring every corner, while also stepping very cautiously as part of me still imagined the floor simply giving out underneath me. Eventually, I returned to the main courtyard, a sweaty, dusty mess. I thanked the caretaker with a handful of somoni, grateful for yet another unique experience on a journey full of them. It was yet another moment that made me appreciate the fact that I chose to follow my own path.

* * *

The next morning, I needed to take care of some logistics before heading on to Turkmenistan. My first stop was at a local Tcell store to get a new SIM card so I could call my guide at the border. Just as I had issues getting a SIM card in Dushanbe, I hit roadblocks in Bukhara. First, the nice English-speaking clerk told me he couldn't sell a SIM card to a foreigner. Seeing my puzzled look, he quickly added that if I went to the main store across town, it should be no problem. Before I had a chance to ask for directions, he offered to drive me there. Feeling particularly trusting of strangers and my own instincts (and desperately needing a SIM card), I followed him outside to his car. However, when we arrived at the other store, the clerk there told me that I had to have a registration stamp from my hotel in my passport. The fact that I had slips of paper with the stamps (as was typical in Uzbekistan, one of the only former Soviet states to cling to this very Soviet-era tradition) didn't matter. My new friend, though, had a solution—he would buy the card for me and register it to his passport. Problem solved.

Ten minutes later, I walked out of the Tcell store with a

new SIM card. We were quite a distance from the Old Town where I was staying, so the clerk offered to drive me back. As he wove through traffic, he asked me about my plans in Bukhara. I explained I was heading to the border first thing in the morning to cross into Turkmenistan. Before I knew it, he was on his phone, calling a friend who drives a taxi and arranging a ride for me—at a lower price than I had been quoted by multiple drivers when I'd asked around. When he dropped me off at my hotel, I thanked him profusely for all his help, and he replied with words that I share with others every chance I get:

"I've been to other countries, and people have helped me. So when people visit my country, I think I should help them. They are my guests."

15

Turkmenistan

As my taxi pulled away from my Bukhara hotel at 7:15 a.m., I asked how far it was to the Uzbekistan-Turkmenistan border at Farab. To my surprise, the driver responded 120 kilometers—much further than I thought. I was supposed to meet my guide, Oleg, on the other side of the border at 9 a.m., and it was clear I would be cutting it close. How had I gotten this wrong? I should've left at least an hour earlier. Despite my meticulous research and planning, it was a reminder that some things could still fall through the cracks.

Sure enough, we pulled up to the Uzbekistan-Turkmenistan border post at 8:45.

As I approached the first building at the border to leave Uzbekistan, a cheerful officer greeted me:

"Tourist?"

"Yes."

"Speak French?"

Puzzled, I shook my head no as I replied, *"Nyet. Ya govoryu po-russki."*

A huge smile came across the officer's face, and he quickly grabbed a blank customs form. Switching from

English to Russian, he asked if I had the form I completed when I arrived in Uzbekistan. I handed that to him, and he immediately started filling in the blanks on the new form for me. Then he gave it to me to complete the rest. Once finished, I showed both forms to another officer sitting behind a window. He chatted with me about my itinerary and where I lived in the United States before stamping my forms without a second glance.

Paperwork in hand, I walked 200 meters to the next building, which was the actual customs checkpoint. Three women and an elderly man stood in front of me as an officer pulled pair after pair of jeans out of several large bags belonging to two men. It seemed they were importing knock off Levis into Turkmenistan. I had a feeling it might take a while. Soon, nearly a dozen truck drivers appeared and, for unclear reasons, they proceeded to the front of the line. The women in front of me didn't object, so I assumed this was the norm. But 10 minutes later, when a group of women arrived and decided to ignore those of us waiting, we all quickly objected.

I approached the friendliest-looking officer and pleaded in a mix of English and Russian that they were cutting in line. Sympathetic to my situation, he pulled me into the glass booth, together with the Uzbek woman in front of me. The waiting continued, though, as the Uzbek woman had some major issues. I tried my best to appear patient as the officer did a lot of scolding and questioning, and she did a lot of pleading and explaining. Finally, it was my turn. The officer asked me to clarify the amount of currency I had on me but ignored my response. Then he yelled out to the officer doing the baggage checks that I was an American tourist. Apparently, that got me out of having my bags checked. I simply picked them from the X-ray machine and moved on. They had searched everyone else in front of me. Leaving the customs building, I nearly missed the minuscule desk that was passport control. Luckily, the officer behind the desk caught me with the familiar *"devushka"* yell, and I stopped to get the all-important stamp out of Uzbekistan.

From there, I walked to an open road that I assumed led to Turkmenistan. Some truck drivers told me it was 1.5 kilometers—there were taxis that shuttled people back and forth, but I unwisely opted to walk. As I passed a huge line of semi-trucks waiting to cross the border, two drivers offered me some watermelon and warned me of "very bad police." I politely declined as I was already an hour late to meet Oleg. With sweat dripping through my light-yellow T-shirt, I finally got to the front of the line of semis and saw only a very small brick building. I thought this would be the beginning of formalities at the Turkmenistan border, but I was wrong. I was still in Uzbekistan.

A tall, fair-skinned officer approached me with a smile, again asking if I spoke French. After repeating the exchange I had leaving Uzbekistan earlier, he inspected my passport and asked in Russian whether I had a Turkmenistan visa. I explained I had a guide waiting for me and that I had an invitation. He went over to a nearby building, and after a short conversation with two officers, he returned, telling me that a taxi would come to take me down the road to the Turkmenistan border for 1,000 som (about 50 cents).

Finally, I reached the building for Turkmenistan passport control. As I did, a tall, muscular Russian man in a white T-shirt and cargo pants approached me—it was Oleg! I was so relieved, I nearly hugged him. Instead, I greeted him with an enormous smile and apologized for my tardiness. Then I stood to the side as Oleg handled everything with my visa. The process seemed difficult enough with him doing it. I was scared to think of how hard it may have been if I had been on my own. The officer asked a lot of questions about my itinerary and seemed generally troubled by me, but he was nowhere near as hostile as the immigration officer had been when I entered Azerbaijan.

Eventually, he put the visa in my passport and handed me an entry card that I would need to carry with me throughout my visit and turn in when I left. The cost of the visa was $85, but I only had $100 bills and they only had $11 in change, so it ended up costing me $89. Then it was on to the X-ray machine and brief questioning by the customs officer, who wanted to know whether I had any religious books, whether I had any drugs, and again, whether I had any religious books (while I assumed they were concerned about non-Islamic materials, Oleg later explained they were trying to keep out Islamic extremism).

Finally, the officer smiled and said in English, "Welcome to Turkmenistan."

* * *

I stared out the window as we cruised along a mostly empty highway through the desert. Turkmenistan was one of the least densely populated countries in the world, with just

10.7 people per square kilometer. After driving through the border town of Farab and then Turkmenabat, I'm not sure we even passed another village until we arrived in the city of Mary about four hours later. Mary was our stop for the night. We checked into a hotel near a busy intersection with a half dozen truck stops. My room was small but clean, and I had a television that was showing the summer Olympics, which was a cultural experience in itself. I had grown up watching the Olympics every four years, my eyes usually glued to the Parade of Nations. Just as I made lists of countries as I spun my globe, I made lists of the countries that marched into the opening ceremonies of the Olympics every four years. It was also fascinating to see how another country covered one of the largest sporting events in the world.

The next morning, we backtracked north to visit what remained of the Silk Road city of Merv. With a population around 200,000 Merv may have been the largest city in the world in the 12th century. It was a convergence point for the northern and southern routes of the Silk Road. Some considered it the capital of the eastern Islamic world. When I visited, it was one of just three UNESCO World Heritage Sites in Turkmenistan and probably the best known, which probably wasn't saying much. Merv was not nearly as well preserved (or restored) as cities like Samarkand and Bukhara in Uzbekistan. A few buildings had been renovated and featured explanatory signs in English, but without Oleg there to guide me, I'm not sure I would have appreciated what I was seeing. The site was also very spread out, making it necessary for us to drive from place to place.

To get an impression of the entire city, Oleg suggested climbing to the top of the walls of the Erk Kala, a seventh-century B.C. fortress that was the oldest part of Merv. From there, I could see the different sections of the former city—the Persian town, the Greek town, the Turk town—each having its own history, creating a layering effect throughout the site. While many of the old city walls had been blown over with sand, I stopped at one wall where the timeworn bricks were still visible. Different-sized bricks revealed the ages of various sections of the wall—the oldest being built in the fourth century B.C., while expansions of the wall dated to the fifth century A.D.—a span of 1,000 years of history right there in front of my eyes.

The most remarkable remains were those of the castle known as the Great Kyz Kala. Originally thought to date to the 11th century, the bricks were of a size used in Persian times, and a sixth-century plate at the Hermitage in St. Petersburg showed a similar structure. Thus, I was likely walking around a building that had been standing for at least 1,500 years. Coming from a country that has only existed for a few hundred years, the feeling of walking on such ancient ground was overwhelming. The fact that it hadn't been restored or overtaken by hordes of tourists was even more powerful.

The Mongols attacked Merv in 1221 and murdered all its inhabitants. A century later, the city was revived, becoming the seat of a Christian archbishopric for the Eastern Orthodox church. It was pulled into Timur's empire, which stretched from modern-day Iraq as far north as the Volga and Ural Rivers in Russia. The Persians later captured Merv, followed by the Emir of Bukhara who, in 1785, destroyed the city and deported the entire population. Decades later, it was abandoned for good. Merv was centuries older than the ancient capital of Ani, which I had visited months earlier, and it served as a solemn reminder that the violence that preceded the desertion of Ani was not unique to the 20th century. Humans have been fighting over religion, land, and power for centuries.

* * *

A few nights later, I lay on my back, gazing up at a sky full of stars, watching the full moon rising in the distance. A light breeze swirled around me, occasionally breaking the silence as it rustled the flaps of my tent. Aside from Oleg in a tent a few feet away, I was completely alone. I wondered who else might be staring at the same sky full of stars as the tune of "Somewhere Out There" played in my head. I wondered if it was possible to get any further away from civilization than I was right then. It was the most at peace I'd felt in months: no Blackberry to check, no emails to read, no blog posts to write, no English to teach, and no onward plans to worry about.

When we'd arrived at the Yangykala Canyon that afternoon, Oleg told me he had only learned of the canyon's existence a few years earlier. Upon seeing pictures of it, he didn't believe it was in Turkmenistan. His admission didn't surprise me. Turkmenistan was known as the "North Korea of Central Asia." Its sparse population was concentrated in the capital of Ashgabat and with no free press, free expression, or even freedom of movement, information about the rest of the country didn't reach most of its inhabitants. On top of that, the Yangykala Canyon was about as remote as you could get. Once we turned onto the rocky unmarked road leading to the canyon, we passed only one other person—a man on a motorbike who likely lived in a small Kazakh village at least an hour away. Oleg said he'd never encountered another person while visiting the canyon—tourist or local.

But there we were, standing on the plateau above the canyon, staring at pink and white rock formations created by an ocean that had existed some 40 million years ago. And there I was that night, camping under a full moon on a canyon plateau in the middle of the desert in Turkmenistan. And for possibly the first time in months, I really wished I wasn't traveling solo. I longed for someone to share the unique experiences with me. Sure, I had Oleg with me, but it wasn't the same. He was my guide and after we bid goodbye at the border a few days later, it was unlikely I would ever see him again. Instead, I yearned to have someone by my side who I could call up 10 years later and say, "Hey, remember that time we camped above that remote canyon in Turkmenistan?"

* * *

I stepped carefully over the faded yellow, green, and red bricks, pausing whenever a spot of turquoise or royal blue caught my eye—fragments of ceramic mixed in with the city ruins. I tried to follow the vague path that seemed to lead over the dirt mounds that once had formed city walls, afraid that one misstep would trigger a mini avalanche of bricks. Eventually, the path took me down the other side of the walls and into the heart of what was once the city of Misrian.

Piles of dirt and bricks surrounded me, the remains of ancient stores and houses. Plants peaked out between the stone and clay, and the ground was conspicuously free of footprints. I spotted more bits of blue and turquoise ceramic, together with broken pieces of orange pottery. In the distance, I could see two large minarets and what remained of a ninth-century mosque. Later that night, as I climbed the crumbling stone stairs of one of the minarets to watch the sunset, I thought about how lucky I was. How many other people, much less tourists, had ever had the chance to enjoy the same view?

The area around Misrian was settled in the third millennium B.C., and from the eighth to 14th centuries, it was a major stopping point for Silk Road caravans traveling from Khorezm (in what is now Uzbekistan) to Ghirkania (now northern Iran). But then the climate changed, and the rivers running near Misrian dried up. And the city that once rivaled Samarkand and Bukhara in prestige and importance was soon abandoned. As I saw firsthand in Uzbekistan, Samarkand and Bukhara ultimately became thriving cities that attract throngs of tourists to their centuries-old mosques and madrassahs, many carefully renovated and restored to their former glory. But Misrian stood quiet and, for the most part, untouched. No buses or marshrutkas or taxis could take me there. Only a four-wheel drive could navigate the dozens of kilometers of bare desert roads, and only a guide like Oleg would know where to go.

When we arrived, the ruins of the city sat open and exposed, with just the foundations of a few buildings fully excavated. There was no ticket office at the entrance and no guards watching over me as I wandered around while Oleg set up our camp. We spent the night camping between the ruins of the inner and outer city walls and woke up to the sight of camels passing in the distance. When was the last time another person had even set foot there? It felt like we may have been the first in years. It was this kind of surreal feeling that made me enamored with traveling off the beaten path in the first place. From Merv to Yangykala to Misrian, I was falling in love all over again with traveling to far-flung places.

* * *

My jaw dropped as Oleg and I drove into the capital city of Ashgabat for the first time. All I needed was green-tinted glasses and I would have sworn I was driving through the Emerald City in *The Wizard of Oz*. Real cities just didn't look like this: gargantuan white marble buildings trimmed in gold, perfectly manicured lawns, and practically empty sidewalks. Pedestrians were conspicuously absent despite it being mid-afternoon on a weekday.

Policemen stood at every corner, by every building, and everywhere in between. They seemed to be on the lookout for three things: people walking where they shouldn't be walking, people trying to take pictures of just about anything, and people driving dirty cars. Yes, it was illegal to drive a dirty car in Ashgabat. I wouldn't have believed it if Oleg hadn't stopped to wash our vehicle a few miles out of town. This was one of several bizarre laws enacted by Turkmen dictator Gurbanguly Berdimuhamedow. Try saying that three times fast.

Taking pictures of nearly every cool-looking building or monument was forbidden, likely a holdover rule from Soviet times. Throughout my trip, I'd been reluctant to photograph government buildings, but in Ashgabat, they seemed to take the Soviet-era prohibition to a new level. This made being a tourist and a travel blogger challenging. Surrounded by buildings that were majestic in their white and gold opulence, I had to restrain myself from whipping out my camera. I heard my fair share of warnings even with my camera tucked in my purse; I was hesitant to risk being spotted pushing the shutter to take a photo. Walking down Turkmenbashy Avenue, I strayed too close to the Presidential Palace complex and an officer swiftly instructed me to cross the street and added that photos were *"nilzya"*—forbidden. The next day, I again got too close to something without realizing it and was reprimanded a second time, this time by two officers who insisted they didn't know Russian and refused to give me directions back to my hotel.

I tried to avoid a third admonishment by asking permission before taking a picture of a tall monument near the Presidential Palace. I didn't want to snap a photo of any of the surrounding buildings—just the tall black and gold column that stood in a circle in the middle of the four-way intersection. But apparently, even asking to take a picture of a non-building was a serious offense because that resulted in more harsh words being hurled at me. After wandering around for another hour, I had to try to engage with the police once again. Ashgabat had wide, busy parkways with few crosswalks and the only nearby underpass was closed. Feeling desperately lost and unable to figure out where to safely cross the street, I nervously approached yet another policeman. Rather than yell at me or rebuke me in any way, he gave me directions and helped me to cross the street—and then complimented me on my Russian and told me to enjoy the rest of my time in Ashgabat.

I did the best I could, but Ashgabat wasn't so much a city to enjoy, but a city to marvel at. I did spend a few hours inside the Nature and Ethnographic Museum, a wing of the National Museum, and was pleasantly surprised to find well-organized displays and explanations in English. In front of the museum, I strained my neck to stare up at the largest flag in the world. Miraculously, no one stopped me when I took not just one but several pictures of it.

I also checked out the Russian Bazaar and strolled around several of Ashgabat's parks—just about the only places in the city that weren't built of white marble and gold and where I could freely take pictures (although I still found myself looking over my shoulder). By my last day, I managed to find a spot that was far enough away for the police to ignore me but close enough that I could get some decent photos of the white and gold buildings using the modest zoom on my camera. I was taking a risk, but it was a calculated one and by that point, I was confident I would get away with it.

* * *

"Is this it?" I asked Oleg as he pulled off the road onto a dirt track. It was nearly 6 p.m. and the hot August sun was still shining bright.

"Yes," he replied with a laugh, noticing how puzzled I looked. We were supposed to be at the infamous Darvaza Gas Crater, but all I saw in every direction were miles of sand. I followed Oleg with a sense of skepticism as he got out of the car. How could we be at the most well-known tourist site in the entire country without so much as a sign to announce its presence?

Suddenly, a gust of wind hit me with so much heat I thought I might be on fire.

"Whoa!" I exclaimed as Oleg gave me a look as if to say, "I told you so."

I inched closer to the crater that had been on fire since 1971, but it wasn't until I reached the edge that I could finally see the rising fumes and the fiery rocks below the surface. As soon as I did, I took a big step back. It was unnerving to realize that nothing stood between me and the 30-meter-deep fire pit. While I appreciated the lack of barriers while camping near the ruins of Misrian, I suddenly longed for something to prevent me from falling to a near-certain death. The rumble of another vehicle interrupted my thoughts, and soon I saw something I hadn't seen in nine days: another tourist.

For me to stay for the 11 days I wanted in Turkmenistan and to be able to both enter from and depart to Uzbekistan, Turkmen authorities required that Oleg accompany me everywhere outside of Ashgabat. On the other hand, the typical tourist—to the extent there is such a thing in Turkmenistan—settled for five days in transit in the country, usually between Uzbekistan and Iran or between Azerbaijan and Uzbekistan, taking the unreliable cargo ferry across the Caspian Sea. As a result, most travelers in Turkmenistan made just two stops: one in Ashgabat and the other at the crater.

It wasn't long before the tourists multiplied. A Japanese guy and his guide set up camp to the left of us. A group of Germans arrived and pitched their tents to our right. Just after nightfall, some Russians showed up and joined the Germans. An hour later, Australians Dave and Doug from Melbourne appeared. They were doing the Mongol Rally on the same route as Adam, Adrian, and Antonio and had planned to camp right next to the crater. After explaining that the fumes from the crater could kill them, I coaxed them into joining the rest of us a few hundred meters away instead. After two nights camping in the desert with only Oleg for company, the Darvaza Gas Crater almost felt congested. But while the masses at major tourist attractions in places like France, Italy, and Turkey annoyed me, I welcomed the "crowd" of a dozen other tourists at Darvaza.

I often felt shy or intimidated around new groups of people, but at the crater, I felt open and at ease, thrilled to see other tourists for the first time in nearly two weeks. I climbed up the highest hill in the vicinity with the Japanese guy to watch the sunset and after dark, I joined Doug and Dave on top of another hill for a different view of the now-glowing crater. We all then took turns snapping pictures of each other around the crater, trying to get the perfect iconic shot of the most popular tourist attraction in the country.

The next morning, I got up early and climbed back up the hill where I'd watched the sunset to catch the sunrise on the other side. As I enjoyed the solitude at the top, I noticed a guy setting up a tripod down below me. I headed over to say hello, and it turned out to be one of the Russian guys. While he was from Novosibirsk, he had studied at St. Thomas University in St. Paul, Minnesota, just miles from where I grew up.

* * *

I sighed as I stared at the line of dozens of people ahead of me. The midday sun beat down on me as I balanced my backpack on my back and daypack on my chest and imagined a wait measured not in minutes but hours. I had spent the morning touring Kunye Urgench with Oleg, arguably the least impressive but most touristy ruins that I visited in Turkmenistan. As much as I enjoyed Oleg's company, 10 days together left me feeling weary of his constant presence. The introvert in me was craving some alone time. I was anxious to cross the border back to Uzbekistan, where a nice, air-conditioned hotel was waiting for me in Khiva.

Suddenly, I felt a tap on my shoulder. It was Oleg telling me to get out of line and follow him. Sure enough, he took me straight up to the front of the line, where I was whisked right through as if I were a VIP. It was a welcome change from my experience crossing in the other direction eleven days earlier. Once I was stamped out of Turkmenistan and said goodbye to Oleg, the VIP treatment continued as I made my way into Uzbek territory. After easily clearing customs, I caught a taxi to Khiva, ready to venture on my own again.

16
Kazakhstan

It was pitch black outside as I tiptoed down the creaky wooden stairs of my guesthouse. I was the only guest, so there was no chance I'd wake anyone, but given the early hour, tiptoeing felt appropriate. The lobby was dark, lit only by the moon shining through a single window. I went to open the door to see if my taxi had arrived and was surprised to discover the door wouldn't budge. I turned the handle left, then right, then left again, but the door remained closed. I squinted in the dark to see if there was a lock I wasn't seeing, but it slowly dawned on me that I may be locked in.

It was just after 5 a.m. and I was in Nukus, Uzbekistan, about three hours north of Khiva. A taxi was supposed to arrive any minute to take me to the train station in Kungrad, where I would catch a train to Kazakhstan, the penultimate stop on my journey through the former Soviet states. After several attempts at booking a ticket from Nukus to Aktau, Kazakhstan on my own, I used a travel agency in Tashkent to make a booking from Nukus to Beyneu, Kazakhstan instead. From there, I would have to either catch another train about 10 hours later or get a pricey taxi to Aktau. But a few days before I arrived in Nukus, I used Twitter to connect with a local named Darik. The owner of a fledgling tourism website focused on the Karakalpakstan region of Uzbekistan, Darik not only showed me around for an afternoon, but he accompanied me to the train station and helped me change my reservation to a train leaving from Kungrad, a short drive outside of Nukus. That train would take me all the way to Aktau. Darik also arranged for a taxi to take me to Kungrad—or so I thought.

With no staff on duty at the guesthouse and no phone number of anyone to call, I rummaged through the desk to find the key to the front door to let myself out. Luckily, it was in the third drawer I opened. Then, as I stood on the steps outside of the guesthouse in the dark, I began to panic, wondering if the taxi would indeed show up. I had the driver's phone number, but I had almost no credit left on my Uzbek SIM card, so I didn't want to call until I was desperate. By 5:45 a.m., when he still hadn't shown up, I made the call. It lasted about 15 seconds and he seemed to confirm that he was on his way. Sure enough, he pulled up 10 minutes later, and he drove so fast that I made it to Kungrad with an hour to spare.

While the train in Kungrad looked just like so many other trains on my journey through the former Soviet states, I found myself with a third-class, or *platzkart*, ticket instead of a bunk in a four-person *kupe* I was used to. This meant my bunk was open to the rest of the car and I could see and hear everything. There was no privacy in *platzkart*. My biggest surprise as I settled into my upper bunk was that every passenger seemed to board the train with as many melons as they could carry. They hauled them in massive plaid plastic bags—several times larger than a grocery bag back home—or under their arms. Then they stuffed the melons wherever they could find room—in storage bins, under tables, or on top of bunks. While I had certainly enjoyed my fair share of fresh melon in Uzbekistan, I was baffled why people needed to transport so many of them into Kazakhstan.

When night fell, wherever there weren't melons, there were people. While I assumed no one could board the train without a ticket, there seemed to be far more people riding the train than there were bunks. Younger children slept two or three in a bed or shared with parents. Older children rolled out flimsy mattresses or blankets and slept on the floor between the bunks. While I lacked the privacy of a closed compartment, I was thankful I at least had an upper bunk so I didn't have to fight anyone over a place to sleep. It wasn't long before I dozed off to the now-familiar *ba-dum, ba-dum, ba-dum* of the train. Again, I wondered what Grandma Dalton would think of all of this?

* * *

As I lay on my king-size bed in an air-conditioned hotel room in Aktau a day later, I flipped through my Lonely Planet guide to Central Asia, trying to figure out how to spend the two days I had in this port city in western Kazakhstan. A section about visa registration jumped out at me. Even though I had a visa to Kazakhstan, I also had to register with the migration police within five days of arriving in the country. According to the book, the migration office in Aktau was open Mondays to Wednesdays, Fridays, and Saturdays from 9 a.m. to noon.

It was Wednesday. I was hoping to do an overnight excursion Friday and Saturday and I would move on to Aralsk by overnight train on Sunday—and Aralsk didn't have a migration office. I needed to register that day. And it was already 11:15. I hurried downstairs, where the receptionist told me that the office was in Microdistrict 3. Aktau didn't have street names—it had micro districts and building numbers. So off I went from my hotel in Microdistrict 1, in search of the office with only my Lonely Planet map to guide me. I made it at 11:47.

As I waited for my documents to be processed, I struck up a conversation with Blanca, a Spanish girl sitting across from me. She spoke English better than I spoke Spanish, and we discovered that we had planned similar itineraries for the upcoming week. My friend Megan, who had traveled through the 'Stans years earlier, had told me that it would be easier to meet fellow travelers once I got to Central Asia. From the Mongol Rally guys in Bukhara to the tourists at the Darvaza Crater to Blanca, it seemed she was correct. Blanca was the first solo female long-term traveler I had met in months, and I welcomed the opportunity to compare notes and share tips.

Unlike me, Blanca had confirmed her plans. She was heading to Beket-Ata the next day. An underground mosque in the middle of the desert and an important place of pilgrimage in Kazakhstan, it was one of the main reasons I wanted to visit Aktau. Blanca relayed that her Couchsurfing host, Andrey, told her she could go by minibus directly from Aktau for just 4,000 tenge (about $27). I was intrigued. I hadn't been able to find a single tour company to take me there. My hotel wanted $800 to arrange for a car and driver. After completing the visa registration process, we walked into the city center together. As we ate lunch at a fast-food restaurant, Blanca suggested we meet up with Andrey that night, so he could give me the details of going to Beket-Ata. Not only did he do that, but he also arranged for me to go as well—and to get picked up directly from my hotel.

Blanca and I both planned to move on to Aralsk and the Aral Sea on Sunday night by train. I had emailed someone who told me he could arrange accommodation and an excursion to the ship cemetery where the Aral Sea used to be, but when I gave him my exact dates, he never replied. I grew nervous that I would arrive in Aralsk early Tuesday morning with no place to stay and be stuck there for the day, possibly with no way to arrange an excursion. Again, Blanca had managed to book a homestay and excursion through a tour company. She quickly reached out to the company and arranged for me to join her.

Finally, it turned out that we both intended to visit the Aksu-Zhabagly Nature Reserve in southern Kazakhstan after the Aral Sea. Yet again, Blanca had already booked a room at a guesthouse and arranged some excursions while I was struggling to get anyone to respond to me. She gave me the name of the place where she was staying. I contacted them, and sure enough, they responded immediately. In less than 24 hours, I went from having no firm plans for my time in Kazakhstan to having a whole week completely mapped out—all because I decided to talk with a stranger, be flexible with my plans, and ignore my inclination to feel like I was imposing.

* * *

The sun was still rising as I climbed into a white minivan in front of my hotel. Blanca was already inside with a group of female Kazakh pilgrims who would be our companions for the five-hour drive into the desert to the underground mosque known as Beket-Ata. Blanca and I were the only non-Kazakh women in the van, but the three women and their children quickly embraced us, asking our names in Russian and introducing themselves with a smile.

Beket-Ata was named for a prominent Sufi leader who built a madrassah and several underground mosques in the Mangistau region of Kazakhstan—far western Kazakhstan, near the Russian border. He died at the age of 63 (also the age at which the Prophet Muhammad died) and he was buried at Beket-Ata. From what I'd read, some considered Sufism to be the "inner, mystical dimension of Islam," while others believed it was outside the sphere of Islam altogether.

Before reaching Beket-Ata, we made a required stop at Shopan-Ata—the underground mosque of another Sufi who was said to have inspired Beket-Ata. There, Blanca and I followed the lead of the pilgrims as they stopped first at the toilets to cleanse themselves and then to a dining hall where we were offered tea with milk and a variety of cookies, candies, and dried fruit. We listened to a prayer and then walked along with the pilgrims past a large cemetery to a small cave that was the actual mosque of Shopan-Ata. Despite our religious differences, Blanca and I were welcomed with open arms. After another prayer, the imam approached us, asking in Russian where we were from. He then explained the history of the mosque, presented us with prayer clothes, and wished us well. I appreciated his approach, only trying to educate us about traditions and history without judgment or an attempt to convert us. It was quite the contrast to the evangelical Christians I spent so much time with growing up. Indeed, no one even asked us what religion we practiced, if any at all.

From Shopan-Ata, we drove two more hours to Beket-Ata. I had imagined it would look something like the cave monasteries or churches I visited in Turkey, Georgia, or Armenia—a series of rooms built into the side of a mountain. The pilgrimage to Beket-Ata was often undertaken as an overnight trip, so I envisioned groups of pilgrims sleeping on mats in large caves with few amenities. On the contrary, we arrived to find a guesthouse that was less than a decade old, with air-conditioned sleeping areas. As we did at Shopan-Ata, we began by visiting the toilets and then sitting down to more tea, cookies, candies, and dried fruit. This confused me as it was Ramadan and I thought all Muslims would be fasting during daylight hours. I wondered if these Sufis did consider themselves outside the realm of Islam as I had read.

After a short rest and another prayer, it was finally time to visit the underground mosque. We followed our group of pilgrims and dozens of others through a brick arch behind the guesthouse and caught our first glimpse of Beket-Ata—far off in the distance, down what appeared to be an almost never-ending set of stone stairs. We methodically descended the stairs under a blazing and unforgiving sun that left me drenched in sweat. I was kicking myself for only bringing a head scarf and not a hat. Every few hundred meters, we found a shelter and enjoyed the slightest amount of shade before pushing on. Shortly before reaching the mosque, I stopped to fill my water bottle with spring water. Only when I was finished did I realize that the pilgrims all carried empty bottles with them that they would not fill until after visiting the mosque. I looked around sheepishly, hoping no one had seen me commit a faux pas by filling mine early.

When we reached the bottom, I was shocked to see that the "underground mosque" was nothing more than a small cave, smaller than the bedroom in my Chicago condominium. I watched as groups of pilgrims ahead of us took turns pushing their way into the cave as others tried to depart. When I finally squeezed into the cave with about 20 other pilgrims to listen to another prayer, it felt even hotter than it had outside. For all the effort we put into getting to the mosque, the whole thing lasted less than five minutes. I'd be lying if I said I didn't feel a bit deflated. I didn't know what I was expecting, but it wasn't what I had just experienced.

Then came the biggest challenge of all: the brutal walk back up the mountain. I lingered longer and longer at each shelter, trying to quench my thirst while conserving water, so I would have enough to last me until I reached the top. I used a mental image of the air-conditioned sleeping room as motivation to keep myself going. Three hours after starting the excursion, I collapsed back onto a mat in the cool room I had been envisioning.

After an extended rest and more tea and snacks, it was time for dinner. The women gathered in one room and the men in another. We sat in small groups around mats on the floor and dug into a communal bowl full of sticky rice and greasy mutton. After eating alone throughout my homestays in Tajikistan, I savored the experience of eating with dozens of Kazakh women. As we ate, several teenage girls approached me and Blanca, anxious to practice their English. We were thrilled to oblige. It was inspiring to hear them talk about their dreams of becoming doctors or lawyers or visiting the United States as we sipped on cups of broth. After a final round of tea, several women handed out pieces of cloth for us to take with us—mine was blue velvet with gold glitter on it, like the material used in many of the traditional Kazakh dresses. This would become one of my most treasured souvenirs.

* * *

As we rode down a bumpy, sandy road through the Kazakhstan steppe, I didn't realize that we were riding over land that was once covered with water. We were speeding toward what is known as the "ship cemetery"—the rusty remains of three ships that used to sail the sea that had mostly disappeared. But during the hour it took to reach the lonely boats, it never occurred to me that the land we were crossing used to be the Aral Sea.

As I got out of the car to take a closer look at the abandoned ships, I kept thinking it should be cloudy. It seemed too sunny, too bright, too happy. I had pictured the Aral Sea in black and white: dark, gloomy, hopeless. Instead, I roamed around shells of boats covered with maritime-themed caricatures and surrounded by grazing cows, all under bright blue skies.

The Aral Sea was once one of the four largest lakes in the world, covering a whopping 68,000 square kilometers (26,300 square miles). But then the Soviets came along in the 1960s and started a massive irrigation project to grow cotton that diverted the rivers that ran into the lake. As a result, the Aral Sea began to shrink and shrink and shrink. By 2007—some 40 years after the Soviet interference began—the Aral Sea covered only 10% of the area it once had.

The near disappearance of the Aral Sea has been called one of the world's worst environmental disasters. The area's once-booming fishing industry was destroyed. Pollution caused myriad health problems, and climate change resulted in hotter and drier summers and colder, longer winters. The population of Aralsk, the city that once stood on the shores of the sea, dipped dramatically. Among those who remained, unemployment levels were high.

All of this was evident within minutes of leaving our homestay in Aralsk. The former port stood just 100 meters away. Cranes still towered over the empty basin, with grass, rocks, and a few large puddles where there should have been waves splashing onto shore. To its credit, Kazakhstan was working to reverse the damage to the north Aral Sea (the south Aral Sea lies in Uzbekistan). In 2005, they completed a dam project that resulted in water levels rising by about 12 meters (40 feet) by 2008. The shoreline, which had once receded to over 60 kilometers from the city of Aralsk, was just 16 kilometers away when we arrived. A small amount of fishing had resumed, but not enough to bring people or jobs back to Aralsk. Some claimed the climate was improving and health issues were decreasing. But considering the newly replenished north Aral Sea covered just 3,300 square kilometers, there was clearly a very, very long way to go.

After visiting the ship cemetery and stopping at the current-day shoreline of the Aral Sea, we returned to Aralsk for lunch. A much-needed afternoon nap gave us relief from the scorching dry heat. By early evening, we decided to venture out to see some of the town but quickly realized there was not much to see beyond the abandoned port. We returned to the homestay for dinner, then caught a taxi to the station for our overnight train.

Here, Blanca and I parted ways as I had booked a *kupe*—or second class—ticket to Shymkent, and she had booked *platzkart*, or third class, as far as Zhabagly. The incoming train only stopped at Aralsk for three minutes, so it was a mad dash to get on the train as soon as it pulled in. I discovered later that because *platzkart* was so full and there were so many people trying to board the train without tickets, they didn't let anyone on, including Blanca. She was left behind.

*   *   *

I arrived in Almaty a few days before my 36th birthday. Turning 36 meant that I was suddenly closer to 40 than ever and that scared me. As I lay in bed in the hotel room I splurged on, I pulled up one of my favorite movies on my laptop: *When Harry Met Sally*. I cringed as I watched the scene with Meg Ryan sitting on her bed in a bathrobe, crying on Billy Crystal's shoulder over a breakup and wailing, "But I'm going to be 40!" Crystal looks at Ryan in surprise and asks when, and she replies matter-of-factly, "Someday." For me, that someday was suddenly a little too close for comfort.

When I was a lawyer in my 20s, 30 seemed far away. I had this idea of who I would be and what I would be doing at 30. I clipped a list from *Glamour* magazine of 30 things I should do before I turned 30, and I think I managed to check off about half. But then 30 came and went. Nothing was how I thought it would be, from my career to my friendships to my love life. As I looked ahead to 40, I didn't want to feel the same disillusionment over where I was at that age as I did about where I'd been at 30.

I had timed my stop in Almaty to coincide with my birthday because it was the same day as Kazakhstan's Independence Day. I figured the city would have a festive vibe and that it would be contagious. But I spent the first 24 hours wallowing in self-pity, wondering what on earth I was doing with my life. That initial somberness eventually turned to reflection as I took time to notice all the positive turns in my life since turning 30. Whatever expectations I had for my future at that age, I likely exceeded them by achieving things I hadn't even imagined possible. If someone had told me when I was 30 that I'd be spending my 36th birthday in Kazakhstan, I wouldn't have believed them.

After feeling like my world was falling apart at age 30, I started running. Over the next few years, I completed five marathons, including the Tallinn Marathon at the beginning of my trip. I started my travel blog and went from not knowing anyone who had quit their job to travel to surrounding myself with new friends who loved travel as much as I did. In the prior year alone, I traveled across Russia on the Trans-Siberian Railway, camped under the stars in Turkmenistan, and bonded with an amazing family in Tajikistan. I drank cognac with a bunch of Georgians, visited places like Chornobyl, the Aral Sea, and Lake Baikal, and improved my Russian tenfold. And I met some incredible people—some who I would likely never encounter again, but some who I hoped would become lifelong friends.

With the end of my trip in sight, I started thinking about what would come next. I had already started applying for jobs back home even though I wasn't that sure what I wanted to do. I wasn't confident that I could build a career as a travel writer or blogger, but did I want to go back to fundraising? And where did I want to end up, back in Chicago or somewhere else? More importantly, what did I want to do beyond finding a new job?

Before I knew it, I had created a list of things to do before I turned 40. Some were task-oriented, like selling my Chicago condominium (something I'd wanted to do before I left but wasn't able to) and paying off my student loans. Many were travel-related, like hiking the Grand Canyon, running the Great Wall Marathon, and seeing the Great Migration in Africa. Others were grander and more idealistic, like finding fulfillment in my career and falling in love. Together, my new list gave me a renewed sense of purpose as I approached my eventual return home. As my friend and fellow blogger Alexis had written so poignantly, I may not have known exactly what direction I was headed, but it felt like forward.

17

Kyrgyzstan

As I sat in a large booth in a small Bishkek diner eating my umpteenth plate of *plov* since arriving in Central Asia, I suddenly heard the unmistakable sound of American English being spoken nearby. I looked up to see that two men around my age had taken seats in the booth adjacent to mine. They were trying to decipher the menu, which was written only in Russian. I glanced over a couple times, hoping I might catch their eye, prompting one of them to say hello first. When that didn't work, I realized if I wanted to make a connection, I would have to take the initiative. I took a swig of orange Fanta and inched over in my booth to close the distance between us. Then, I leaned over even further as I asked, "Excuse me, where are you from?"

"New York," said the taller, blond one with wire-rimmed glasses.

"San Francisco," said the shorter one with Asian features.

They introduced themselves as Scott and Jay, two friends traveling through Kyrgyzstan and Tajikistan for a couple weeks. This made them a rarity in a part of the world where the only travelers seemed to be long-term travelers from Europe or Australia. We quickly hit it off and set off to explore Bishkek together. It was the last Central Asian capital I would visit on my trip and I felt like I may have saved the best for last. From getting lost in the chaotic Osh Bazaar to wandering through the sprawling Ala-Too Square, Bishkek had everything I had grown to love in a city.

While I visited dozens of markets and bazaars while traveling, Bishkek's Osh Bazaar was one of my favorites. The bazaar was a cornerstone of Central Asian life—the beating heart of any city or town. A maze of narrow alleys and crowded stalls, Central Asian bazaars overwhelmed the senses and reeked of chaos. They were where centuries-old traditions came to life. Farmers came from miles around to hawk their fruits or vegetables—apples, grapes, cherries, melons, peppers, carrots, potatoes and more. The aroma of spices floated far and wide. Butchers showed off fresh meat—perhaps a little too fresh for the squeamish. Vendors stocked beauty products, school supplies and even electronic goods and SIM cards. Enterprising men and women also provided almost any service imaginable. Need a dentist? Go to the bazaar. Need a pharmacist? Go to the bazaar. Indeed, I returned to the bazaar on my own the next day and emerged with a haircut, manicure and pedicure.

Having two new friends to experience Bishkek with made my experience in the city even better. At the end of the day, we exchanged email addresses and tentatively planned to meet up in Osh, a city in southern Kyrgyzstan that I already had on my itinerary. I had booked a flight to Osh for two days later, while they were planning to take a shared taxi the next day—at least a 10-hour journey. I immediately regretted planning so far ahead and wished I could instead join them for the road trip to Osh. By the time I arrived in the city, they had already moved on to Sary-Tash, a popular stop on the way to Tajikistan.

* * *

The Karakol Sunday animal market was already in full swing when I arrived around 8 a.m. on a Sunday morning. Karakol was on the far eastern tip of Lake Issyk Kul. I had taken a taxi from my guest house to visit the market—something I considered a "can't miss" in Karakol. After paying my taxi driver, I walked past dozens of cars and taxis parked just outside of the market area; most were likely used to transport smaller animals to the market, or they would be used to carry purchases away. I quickly realized that animals were grouped together in sections, giving a sense of order to the otherwise frenzied atmosphere around me. Young children stood encircled by half a dozen young goats. Men struggled to load finicky sheep into a flatbed truck. Tourists roamed among it all, cameras in tow.

Soon, the bustling sheep and goats around me gave way to large, lazy cows. The crowds thinned out, and things felt slightly more subdued. A small group of men surrounded an enormous cow, taking pictures as if they were tourists, too. I made my way to the back of the cow section, only to discover a half dozen piglets for sale—a couple in a small cage on the ground and several others eating heartily in the trunk of an old Lada. I initially saw the animal market as a novelty, an experience unique to Central Asia or Kyrgyzstan. But as I ogled the adorable piglets, I realized the market wasn't all that different from the livestock barns at the Minnesota State Fair back home.

While I was mostly ignored as I strolled through other parts of the market, once I moved on to the area with the horses, I drew a lot of attention. The Kyrgyz men seemed to get a kick out of my presence, posing on horseback and trying to cajole me into trying out a horse. I declined with a smile and a "*nyet*," not having the words in Russian to explain that I had been thrown off a horse at camp when I was a child. The thought of getting on another one terrified me. A few minutes later, as I headed back toward the goats and sheep, a man tried to convince me I needed to buy some sheep. Again, I smiled and shook my head, "*nyet*."

I initially thought it was odd that merchants were trying to sell me livestock as a tourist, but the owner of my guesthouse told me about a couple who bought two horses at the market, together with all the necessary riding gear, and then spent a few weeks exploring Kyrgyzstan by horseback. When their time in the country was up, they managed to sell the horses near the Kazakhstan border, making enough to cover almost the entire cost of their trip. For me, I was just happy to spend a couple hours among the animals, getting a closer look at traditional Kyrgyz life. Indeed, some of my favorite parts of my journey through the former Soviet states were the hours I spent wandering through markets, bazaars, parks and shopping centers, getting a feel for everyday life.

* * *

I shivered as I walked back to my guesthouse just outside the center of Karakol the next night. As daylight faded, I tried to navigate the dirt roads with no streetlights to show me the way. The cool, rainy weather in the town of 65,000 had come as a surprise after spending the prior two months sweating my way through 100-degree temperatures in the rest of Central Asia. I was thankful I'd been able to buy a couple pairs of jeans in Almaty, but I worried about whether I had the right clothing for a multi-day hike in the mountains, which was supposed to be up next on my itinerary.

I had planned a three-day trek around Song Kul Lake with the help of the Community Based Tourism (CBT) coordinator in Bishkek. Similar but unrelated to CBT Azerbaijan, CBT in Kyrgyzstan helped connect tourists with local homestays and guides throughout the country. The coordinator in Bishkek referred me to the local CBT coordinator in the town of Kochkor. Located on the far western shore of Lake Issyk Kul, Kochkor was the jumping-off point for trips to Song Kul. He initially responded by saying he would work on arranging everything, but then I never heard from him again.

As I was waiting to arrange my trip to Song Kul, I talked to others at my guesthouse about the conditions in the mountains. I heard time and time again how cold it could get, especially at night, and how quickly the weather could change. With my meager summer wardrobe from traveling in the desert all summer, I suddenly felt horribly unprepared. My visits to the lone sporting goods store in Karakol and to the central market to find warmer clothes were unsuccessful.

Never one to easily abandon my plans, I decided to press on to Kochkor. Then, the night before I planned to head to Kochkor, I was leaning over to pack up my things when I suddenly aggravated the sacroiliac joint in my lower back—an issue I had in the past that caused a sharp pain to shoot down my hip and linger for hours, even days. Now, I wondered if I physically would be able to handle a three-day trek, regardless of the weather.

I had a growing feeling of trepidation as I boarded a marshrutka headed to Balykchy, where I would catch a shared taxi to Kochkor. I told myself that, at the very least, I could find a homestay for the night and try to arrange something through another local travel agency if CBT wasn't ready for me. And, at the very worst, I could head back to Bishkek. A few hours after leaving Karakol, my marshrutka pulled into a small parking lot in the town of Bokonbaevo on the southern shore of Lake Issyk Kul.

After everyone else piled out of the crowded minivan, the driver informed me that I was the only one going as far as Balykchy. He didn't want to go all the way there just for me, so he arranged for a shared taxi to take me the rest of the way instead. I reluctantly piled my things into the trunk of a rickety-looking station wagon and sat down to wait for it to fill up with enough passengers to leave. As I glanced around from my seat in the back of the station wagon, I noticed a sign on one of the buildings adjacent to the parking lot. It was an advertisement for CBT Bokonbaevo, and it included a phone number.

I got out of the taxi and called the number on the sign. The English-speaking coordinator told me they could arrange a homestay and excursion for me in Bokonbaevo the next day. She could meet me at their office in 15 minutes to finalize plans. I grabbed my things out of the taxi and told the driver that plans had changed. I was staying in Bokonbaevo.

Twenty minutes later, I met not only the coordinator at the office but also a group of three French tourists: Beatrice, Max, and Samuel. They had also just come from Karakol. We quickly realized that Beatrice and I had a short conversation in a café there a couple days earlier. When traveling in countries like Kyrgyzstan, everything tends to cost less with more people involved, so after a brief discussion in which we mutually decided we were compatible enough to spend the next 24 hours together, we booked as a group of four to watch an eagle hunting demonstration and stay at a yurt camp on the shore of Lake Issyk Kul that evening.

At the yurt camp, we met a German anthropology student who took us to Manjyly-Ata the next morning, a holy site and place of pilgrimage with sacred springs. The site wasn't mentioned in any of my guidebooks, and I struggled to find any information about it after our visit. We joined a Kyrgyz family for lunch shortly after we arrived. Then, we walked through the valley of Manjyly-Ata, visiting several different springs along the way. Each spring was said to have specific healing powers. The Ilim spring was to gain knowledge and insight, while the Bala spring would help with infertility. The Bugu Ene spring was said to cure liver and eye diseases and the Aziz Bulagy spring would cure headaches, anxiety and depression. The Manjyly-Ata spring would help with cardiovascular and skin diseases. None of us felt confident enough to drink the spring water, but visiting each of the springs was no less fascinating.

We were all supposed to move on later that day. I was

going to Kochkor to try to salvage my hiking trip to Song Kul Lake, Max was returning to Bishkek, and Beatrice and Samuel were going back to Karakol to trek in the Tian Shan Mountains. But by the time we returned to Bokonbaevo, it was too late to secure onward transportation. We spent another night together, and by Wednesday morning, Beatrice convinced me to return to Karakol with her and Samuel to go hiking there. I gave up on Kochkor and Song Kul Lake altogether.

While I initially thought Beatrice and Samuel were long-time friends (or more) traveling together, it turned out that Beatrice and Max knew each other from working for an NGO in Vietnam, and they had just encountered Samuel a few days earlier. We all got along well enough, although I occasionally felt awkward as they rambled in French to each other, and I couldn't understand a word. I experienced this throughout my journey as I stayed at hostels largely populated by French- and German-speaking travelers. They would speak English to me when they wanted to but spent more time talking to each other in their native languages. I promised myself that when I returned home, I would learn French.

Upon returning to Karakol, we met up with Usan, a Kyrgyz guy Beatrice met earlier. He knew the mountains well and would join us hiking in Jeti Oguz the next day. Usan spent the afternoon showing us around what little there was to see in Karakol. That night, Beatrice, Samuel, and I went out for dinner and then to a bar called the Caravan Café. Not uncommon in the former Soviet Union, the servers didn't really understand the concept of a mixed drink, so our attempts to order vodka and soda or gin and tonic resulted in orders of vodka or gin shots instead. After a few shots, Beatrice started pouring her heart out to me, rambling on about unrequited feelings for Max and an interest in Usan. I suddenly understood why she pushed so hard for me to return to Karakol with her; I could occupy Samuel while she was connecting with Usan. I can't say I minded; I thought Samuel was cute.

As the night went on, a table of Kyrgyz 20-somethings invited us to join them and started buying us shots. We soon moved to the dance floor, where the Kyrgyz girls egged me on to dance with Samuel. Embarrassed by the attention and feeling self-conscious because I had no idea if Samuel was interested in me, I tried to laugh them off. But then, as a slow song started to play, Samuel grabbed me by the hand and pulled me close to him, erasing any doubts. The Kyrgyz girls stood nearby, making hearts with their fingers. Beatrice sat in our booth, catching my eye and giving me a nod of approval.

* * *

I woke up to the feeling of fur rubbing against my face and tiny claws scratching at my chest. As I opened my eyes, I could feel my head throbbing, and for a moment, I wasn't quite sure where I was. The tiny orange kitten snuggled against my neck reminded me: I was in a yurt camp just outside the center of Karakol. The kitten had befriended me the day before. My little orange friend, however, could not tell me how I got myself back to the camp after far too many vodka shots the night before. I slowly sat up in my sleeping bag and looked around. Samuel was snoring next to me and Beatrice was out cold a few feet away. I crawled to the entrance to the yurt and unzipped the door to get some fresh air. Instead, I caught a whiff of the regurgitated remains of the previous night's meal. I immediately suspected they were mine.

Breakfast was an awkward affair as none of us were entirely sure of everything that happened after we left the Caravan Café. The more Beatrice and Samuel spoke to each other in French, the more I was convinced they were talking about me. Once Beatrice left to finish getting ready for the day, Samuel and I had an even more awkward conversation about why we woke up next to each other. As much as I felt like there was a mutual attraction between us the night before, I wondered how much of that was the vodka and how much was the fact that I just happened to be there. No amount of traveling the world could erase my constant insecurities when it came to members of the opposite sex.

Despite our hangovers, we were determined not to waste our last day in Karakol. We stuck to our plan to go hiking in Jeti Oguz. But before we did, Beatrice insisted we return to the Caravan Café to try to settle our bill from the previous night. The one thing we all agreed on at breakfast was that none of us paid before leaving. As the only one in the group who could speak any Russian, I volunteered to explain the situation to the staff and ask how much we owed.

"*Privet. My byli zdes' proshloy noch'yu. Ya dumayu, chto ushli ne oplativ.*" [Hello. We were here last night. I think we left without paying.]

The woman standing before me gave me a puzzled

look and said she would get the server who was working the night before.

When the server appeared, I explained again to her that I thought we had left without paying. She shook her head.

"*Nyet. Vash schyot byl oplachen*," she assured me our check had been paid.

"*Ty uveren?*" I asked. Are you sure?

"*Da*," she replied with an amused smile.

"*My ne mogli vspomnit'. Slishkom mnogo vodki*," I responded with a laugh. Clearly, our bill had been taken care of. The best I could do at that point was admit we had too much vodka and couldn't remember.

She gave me a hearty laugh, and I told Beatrice and Samuel we were good to go. We went outside to catch a taxi to Jeti Oguz.

* * *

I sat in the passenger seat of a shared taxi to Bishkek, replaying the past week in my head. For the first time in 13 months, I'd let myself be completely spontaneous, changing my plans not after hours or days of deliberation but on a whim. It was an incredible, but unfamiliar feeling.

While many people get a rush out of spontaneity and savor flexibility, I was always most comfortable when I had plans. I didn't deal well with uncertainty. Indeed, many aspects of planning for my trip were a challenge because there was so much I didn't know. I didn't know if or when my condo would sell, which would have a huge impact on my ability to travel long-term in the first place. I didn't know if Russia would approve my application for a three-month business visa. In a pre-Obamacare world, I couldn't apply for worldwide medical insurance until 30 days before I left and then I had to scramble when my application was initially denied. And less than a month before my departure, I still didn't know the identities of the families with whom I would be living in Russia. I found all the not knowing incredibly stressful.

True to form, I initially planned out my itinerary down to the day. I did so primarily to come up with a budget; I needed to have an idea of how much the whole adventure was going to cost me so I would know how much I needed to save. That, in turn, determined when I would be ready to leave. I spent countless hours poring through guidebooks and websites coming up with an estimate of how much time I might want to spend in each country, which cities I might like to visit and what sites I'd like to see, how much a typical hostel or guesthouse would cost and what the average meal might run. I threw all this information into a massive spreadsheet, and according to the spreadsheet, as of two weeks before my departure, my trip would last exactly 319 days. And then I declared in a blog post that I would do my best not to follow it:

"If I learn anything on this trip, I hope I will learn to be more flexible and spontaneous. I hope I will allow myself to throw the itinerary out the window once in a while and even if I have plan A in my head, I hope I will be happy resorting to plan B or C or even D. Even better, I hope I can learn to be content sometimes going without a plan altogether."

Of course, I had changed things up occasionally. When things didn't turn out as I'd anticipated with my homestay and volunteer program in St. Petersburg, I decided to cut my time in Moscow in half. I stayed an extra five days in St. Petersburg once the homestay ended and added in a few days in Veliky Novgorod on my way to Moscow. I made a detour to Poland over the holidays and then canceled plans to visit Krakow when I wasn't feeling it and stayed in Warsaw for a week longer than planned. I took another detour to Italy and then Turkey before picking up my planned route again in Georgia and then changed things up again to return to Armenia for a week. In each case, though, I carefully considered my options and researched alternatives before making any decisions.

Now, as I wrapped up one of the most enjoyable weeks of my trip, I realized that some of my most memorable experiences transpired when I let myself be flexible and change my plans on a whim, not after hours or days of thinking about it. The best moments materialized when I let go of expectations and lived in the moment. If I had any regrets, it was that I didn't live in the moment more often. I was always thinking about what was next.

I also couldn't believe my trip was ending. Thirteen months on the road, in 19 countries. Had I accomplished anything I set out to? I wasn't entirely sure. It is sometimes hardest to see what is right in front of you. My journey home would take me back to Riga for a couple days and then to a travel blogging conference in Spain before a final series of flights back to Chicago. As I boarded the flight from Riga to Barcelona, "Good Riddance (Time of Your Life)" by Green Day started playing. As I quietly whispered the lyrics, tears started rolling down my cheeks. Despite all the ups and downs, I absolutely had the time of my life.

* * *

"Well, it looks like you've been gone for a while," observed the officer sitting behind the passport control desk at the Atlanta airport.

"Yes, 13 months," I said with a smile.

He looked at me inquisitively before asking a series of questions: Where did I go? Who "sponsored" me? What did I do? Why?

I answered, apparently to his satisfaction, and then he closed my passport, stamped my customs form and handed both back to me.

"Welcome home."

Epilogue

"Cheers," we said in unison as we clinked our matching glasses of Pinot Grigio together, smiling yet avoiding the kind of direct eye contact that might signal romantic interest.

We had met only 30 minutes earlier. I inadvertently followed him up the stairs toward the private room at the Washington, D.C. bar hosting my law school alumni group. It was my first event after relocating to D.C. from Chicago three months earlier, and I was hoping to make a good impression on whoever I met. Three years after returning from my journey across the former Soviet Union, I finally landed my dream job, fundraising for the National Geographic Society. I moved to D.C. just six weeks later. My network in D.C., though, was limited to a former colleague at my first law firm, a short-term college roommate, and an acquaintance who was too curmudgeonly to count on for much of a social life. I was eager to meet new friends. Nearly 20 pounds lighter than when I'd arrived in D.C. and fresh off a half marathon personal best that weekend, I was also brimming with confidence.

We independently said hello to our host and collected our name tags before colliding at the bar.

"Hi, I'm Katie," I said, offering my hand with the formality that I'd come to expect from any event involving lawyers.

"Evan," he said as he clasped my hand in his. I glanced down quickly, noting the lack of a ring on his finger. He looked familiar, but I couldn't place him as we fell into typical networking dialogue:

"What do you do?"

"How long have you been in D.C.?"

"When did you graduate?"

It turned out that our time in law school overlapped by one year. He insisted he recognized me, and I played along, not wanting to give him any reason to end the conversation. By the time we toasted with newly full glasses of wine, we had moved on from the mundane to sharing favorite sports memories and travel tales.

"Where's your next big trip?" he asked with a genuine curiosity that I'd rarely heard since returning from my year overseas.

"I have two coming up," I replied cautiously, knowing that this could be a make-or-break moment. "I'm running the Great Wall Marathon in China in May and then going to Kamchatka in the fall."

"Kamchatka!" Evan said with a wide grin. "Like in Russia? That's awesome."

And with that, I was smitten.

When I returned to Chicago after my career break trip, it was nearly impossible to meet a guy who could appreciate my wanderlust and independence. A stint as one of the *Chicago Reader's* "most eligible singles" led to just a single lackluster date. My casual mentions of "that time I was in Uzbekistan" were met with puzzled looks. Guys on dating apps who claimed to love to travel just loved to lie on the beach in Miami or hang out at Vegas casinos. My admittedly random litmus test soon became whether a guy had heard of Russia's Kamchatka Peninsula, the number one spot on the list of places I wanted to visit before turning 40. Evan was the first to pass the test.

Our first date was two weeks later. We met purportedly for happy hour on a Thursday night in DuPont Circle but soon moved on to my favorite Lebanese place in Woodley Park for dinner. A bottle of wine and plenty of meze later, we found ourselves a few doors down, sitting in a nearly empty bar, watching the final minutes of the first round of March Madness. My casual hand on his shoulder led to his hand on my knee and, eventually, him leaning in for a highly anticipated kiss.

As soon as we were seated at the restaurant for our second date a couple weeks later, he blurted out, "Just so you know, I have kids."

I was almost 40, so this did not exactly surprise me. I was more concerned with the answer to the question I posed right back to him:

"Are you...married? Divorced? Separated?" I inquired, bracing myself for the answer while clearly recalling the lack of a ring on his finger the night we'd met.

"Divorced," he replied. "Since November." If he saw me breathe a huge sigh of relief, he didn't let on. I thought I could handle dating someone with kids. But if he had been separated or married, I would've walked out the door.

His kids were five and eight, about the same ages as my brother and I were when our parents divorced. I clearly recalled both of their post-divorce forays into dating before they each eventually remarried. While I'd never dated a guy with kids and had never really wanted any kids of my own, I soon became determined to do everything right while dating a divorcee.

In my mind, that meant being as understanding as possible. He was still working out his custody arrangement and told me his ex could be unpredictable. I was also traveling for my new job every other week, so it seemed completely normal to me that we only saw each other once every few weeks. I never questioned the fact that we always went out in my neighborhood, which was far more convenient for me than crossing the river to where he lived in Alexandria. I didn't think twice when he explained he couldn't stay the night because he had to get home to the babysitter. How many times did my dad leave my brother and me with a babysitter while he took out our potential future stepmother?

The next several months consisted of sporadic downtown happy hours, Saturday afternoons watching sports at my neighborhood bar, and late nights at the jazz club around the corner from my apartment. While I harbored hopes that we would make things official and call each other boyfriend and girlfriend, I was more wary of ruining a good thing by pushing him too hard. I often felt like I lost Patrick by trying to get too serious, too fast, and I didn't want history to repeat itself. I had a blast every time we were together, and my travel schedule didn't allow us to see each other that much more often anyway. I reasoned that between seeing me and spending time with his kids, he couldn't possibly have any extra time for anyone else.

We spent most of the summer apart as we both

crisscrossed the globe for work and for pleasure, never landing in D.C. at the same time for almost three months but texting at least a few times a week. When our travel schedules settled down, we started spending full weekends together—a sure sign to me that maybe, just maybe, he was finally ready to get serious. He flew back from visiting his parents in Michigan in time to join me for a Cubs-Nationals baseball game, wearing a Cubs hat to humor me. We spent a lazy Sunday morning in bed, skipping a 10-mile race we had both signed up to run because it was raining. When the skies cleared, we walked arm in arm to the neighborhood diner for blueberry pancakes, something that had become routine. By the time we kissed goodbye, I was already thinking about how we would celebrate his birthday together two weeks later.

* * *

As I walked out of the Belorusskaya station in central Moscow, a sense of familiarity washed over me, yet almost nothing was the same. It had been five years since I'd left this same station, struggling to carry my oversized backpack as I trudged along snow-covered sidewalks in search of my hostel. That backpack was long gone, replaced by a carry-on-sized suitcase that rolled smoothly behind me. I would be spending the next two nights in an upgraded suite at the Moscow Marriott Grand Hotel instead of a loud, crowded hostel dorm room. Instead of the gray skies of October and November, I was met by August sunshine. Indeed, as I wandered down Tverskaya Street to Red Square, I relished the sunshine that had eluded me five years earlier.

The political situation around Russia had changed significantly since I'd visited in 2011. After invading and annexing Crimea in 2014, the country found itself facing international sanctions. As a result, the ruble crashed, and a trip to Kamchatka that previously had seemed out of reach suddenly cost half as much. By the time I flew from D.C. to Moscow in August 2016, the Russian president, Vladimir Putin, was the center of speculation around then-candidate Donald Trump and the approaching U.S. presidential election. Evan worked for a member of Congress and warned me somewhat ominously that I needed to be careful. Assume your hotel room is bugged, he told me. Only connect to the internet with a VPN. I thought he was overreacting, but I took his warnings as a sign he cared.

Two days later, I boarded a flight from Moscow to Petropavlovsk-Kamchatksy, the largest city on the Kamchatka Peninsula in far eastern Russia. Like many people, I first heard of Kamchatka while playing the board game *Risk*. I became intrigued by the idea of visiting it as I planned my career break trip, but I lacked the time or the money at that time to add it to my itinerary. When I made my list of things to do before I turned 40 while sitting in my Almaty hotel room, visiting Kamchatka was near the top. I arrived with just days to spare.

The next week was a stark contrast to my first time in Russia. Although I had never set foot in Kamchatka, it felt comfortable and familiar. The Russian language skills that I hadn't used in four years came back quickly, and I spoke with a confidence I lacked the first time around. I was traveling solo but had booked a tour, so I was meeting new people each day, most of whom were also intrepid travelers like me. We clicked quickly. When my planned helicopter tour to a remote part of the peninsula to see brown bears was delayed due to weather, I didn't stress or get upset. I accepted the change in plans and then felt a sense of relief when we were able to make the trip a few days later. Russia may have changed in the years since my first visit, but so had I.

After returning from my career break trip in 2012, I wrote for more than a dozen travel websites and became a regular contributor to one major site, writing about Chicago, Russia, and the Baltics. My blog appeared on lists of top travel blogs attracting thousands of visitors each month, something I could never have imagined when I first started. I entertained five job offers within three months of returning, including a job at a high-end travel agency. Ultimately, I realized I didn't want travel to be my job. I was afraid it might lose its luster if it became something I had to do instead of something I wanted to do.

I soon invested in a DSLR camera and learned about travel photography on a three-week photography and hiking tour in the Nepal Himalayas. I traveled to Bulgaria solo for my 37th birthday and used my Russian skills to read Bulgarian and occasionally chat up taxi drivers. I ventured to West Africa for the first time, visiting Mali during an Ebola outbreak and Burkina Faso just weeks after a military coup. I hiked the Grand Canyon rim-to-rim and took the train from California to Chicago, checking off two more items on my to-do list. I trekked the Peaks of the Balkans trail through Kosovo, Montenegro, and Albania and participated in the largest road race in Africa, the Great Ethiopian 10K in Addis Ababa. I also hosted visitors from the former Soviet Union through a U.S. State Department program in Chicago, opening my home to Nino from Georgia and Olga from Belarus just as so many had opened their homes to me.

When my dream job presented itself three years after I returned from my career break trip, I didn't hesitate to pack up everything and move to Washington, D.C. The opportunity to work in fundraising at National Geographic felt like all the pieces of the puzzle were finally falling into place. The "ah-ha" moment I had been seeking finally arrived. I was hired as a planned giving officer, working with donors who would include NatGeo in their estate plans. In doing so, I would draw on my legal training and former career as a tax lawyer, as well as my more recent experience in fundraising. The job gave me the opportunity to travel around the U.S. for about two weeks every month and the chance to meet with donors who loved travel as much as me.

As I sat alone at a table in the nicest restaurant in Petropavlovsk-Kamchatsky on my 40th birthday, I realized that I was probably more comfortable with who I was than ever before. After decades of trying to be an extrovert, I'd accepted my inner introvert. I savored my nights home alone, and I no longer cared if someone thought I was weird for staying in on a Friday night. I was no longer intimidated by the idea of attending an event solo, and I didn't feel self-conscious sitting at a bar by myself or at a restaurant alone. While I would never call myself religious or even spiritual,

I was beginning to really believe that things happened for a reason and that everything would work out in the end.

* * *

I froze as I heard the buzz of my iPhone in my purse. Weeks had passed since Evan neglected to invite me to spend his birthday with him, and it had been nearly two months since we'd shared blueberry pancakes at the neighborhood diner. Not only were his texts coming with less frequency, but he avoided making new plans to see me. While I would've preferred having a conversation with him in person, he was making that impossible. I did what I'd done with guys so many times before: I poured out my heart by email. Deep down, I already knew what his response would be; I just needed closure so I could move on. He gave me that in a text message confirming I was right in my suspicion that things were over. He asked me to forgive his inability to be better while encouraging me to move forward and take care of myself.

I wiped away a single tear, sad to lose someone to whom I'd given more of myself than anyone in the past. But this time, I knew it wasn't my fault. It was him, it was the timing, it was the overall situation. On top of that, I was no longer the woman who spent months questioning what she could've done differently. I was no longer the woman crying herself to sleep, wondering why she wasn't fill-in-the-blank enough for a man. While I still wanted a relationship, I knew I didn't need one to be happy. In the meantime, I was quite content to fly solo.

Acknowledgments

This book has been more than a decade in the making. It may be one of the hardest and scariest things I've ever done (which is saying a lot!). It would not have been possible without the advice, encouragement and inspiration of all those listed below.

First and foremost, thank you to my parents, Phil Aune and Kate Lowe, and my stepmother Beth Aune, for supporting my decision to quit my job back in 2011 to travel. Even if you didn't fully understand it, you never tried to discourage me and you did what you could to help me along the way.

Thank you to my high school Western Civilization teacher George Kimball and my college professor Vicki Hesli for unknowingly feeding my fascination with all things Russian and Soviet.

Thank you to those who initially inspired me to take a "career break" to travel and gave me the tools to do so: Sherry Ott, Michaela Potter, Lisa Lubin and Megan Kearney. A special thank you to Sherry for hiring me to manage the *Meet, Plan, Go!* website while I was on the road so I could extend my trip three months longer than planned.

Thanks to David Berghof of StanTours for his patience in advising me for nearly three years about traveling in Central Asia before I finally made it there.

Thank you to Matt Kepnes for giving me my first big break in travel blogging and providing invaluable advice as I struggled through writing this book and preparing to publish it.

Thank you to everyone who followed my journey in real time back in 2011 and 2012. Your comments and emails meant so much and often kept me going. And thank you to everyone whose names appear within the pages of this book (real or otherwise). You are all an integral part of my story and I'm grateful for having met you.

Thank you to Audrey Murray for reinvigorating me to finish this book through the publication of your book, *Open Mic Night in Moscow*.

Thank you to my women's writing group, brought together by Politics & Prose and Natasha Scripture and carried on by our mutual love of writing. Without all of you, I may have put my manuscript back on the shelf and let it sit for another five years: Jennifer Browning, Carolina Espinal, Jerilyn Libby, Christina McAlister, Kerry Porter and Jennifer Tepper.

A huge thank you to my editor Nancy Pile, who saw things in my story (and in me) that I failed to see myself. You were instrumental in shaping it into the book it is today. And thank you to Fien Kiestelyn for your encouragement and introducing me to Nancy.

An enormous thank you to my volunteer beta readers who took the time out of their busy lives to read an earlier draft of my manuscript and offer honest praise and constructive criticism: Tania Cohen, Jennifer Dumas, Ali Garland, Andy Luten, Brianne Miers, Cali O'Connor and Aaron Shapiro.

Finally, thank you to Bruce Tria for his amazing cover design, Antonio Tavares for the illustrated maps of my journey, Adam Daniels for taking my headshot for the back cover and Karina Grosheva for checking my Russian translations.

About the Author

Katie R. Aune is a recovering tax attorney who has worked in nonprofit and higher ed fundraising for more than a decade while also dabbling in travel blogging and writing. Despite not traveling overseas for the first time until she was 25, she has been to nearly 70 countries and all seven continents. Born and raised in Minnesota, Katie is currently based in Washington, D.C. and has a habit of rooting for sports teams that find ways to lose in devastating fashion. You can find her on social media as @katieaune and read more about her travels at katieaune.com.

Made in the USA
Middletown, DE
20 November 2023